CREATURES OF THE NIGHT

&

CLOWNING AROUND

HORROR COLORING BOOK

CREATURES
Of The Night

Horror Coloring Book

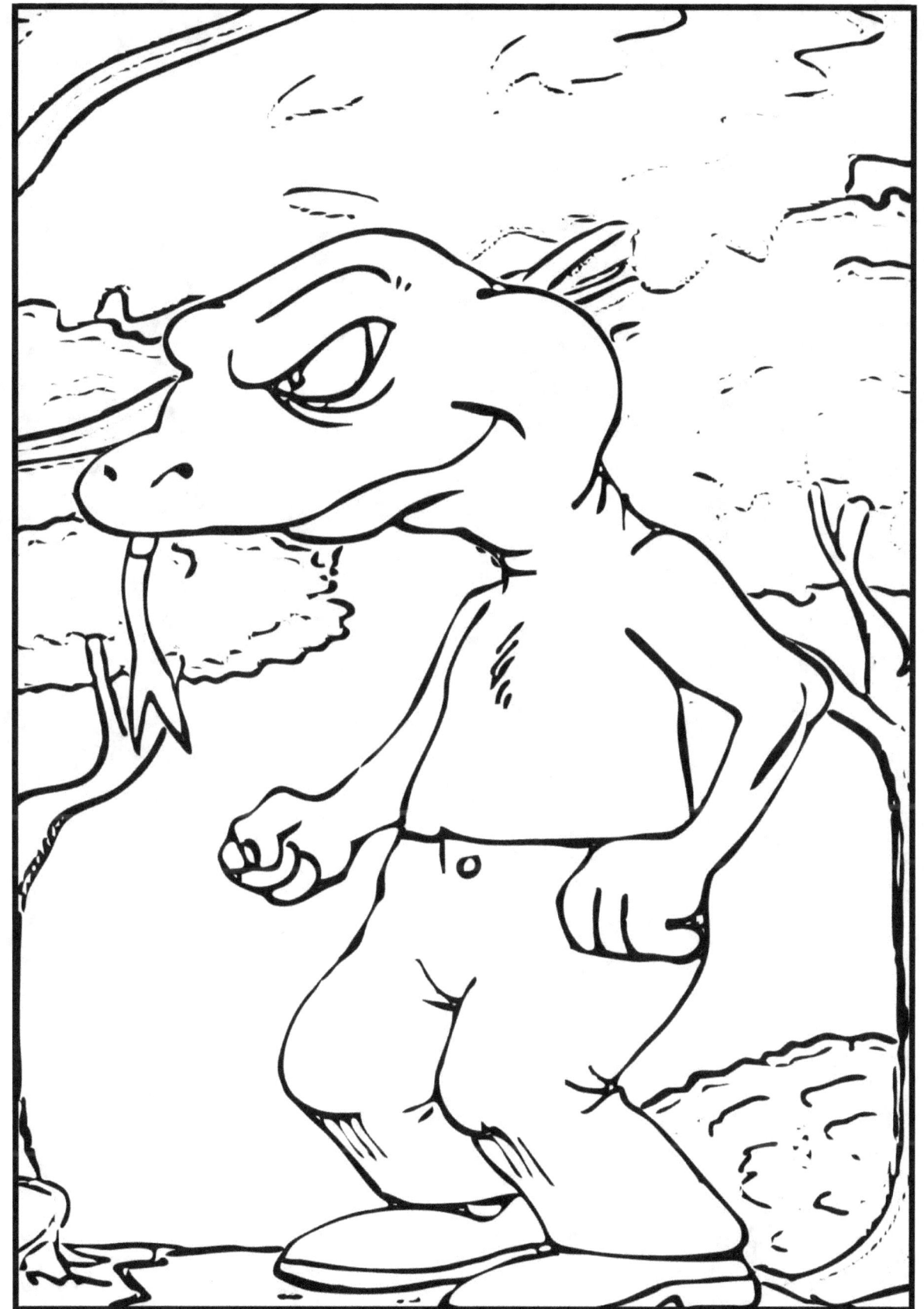

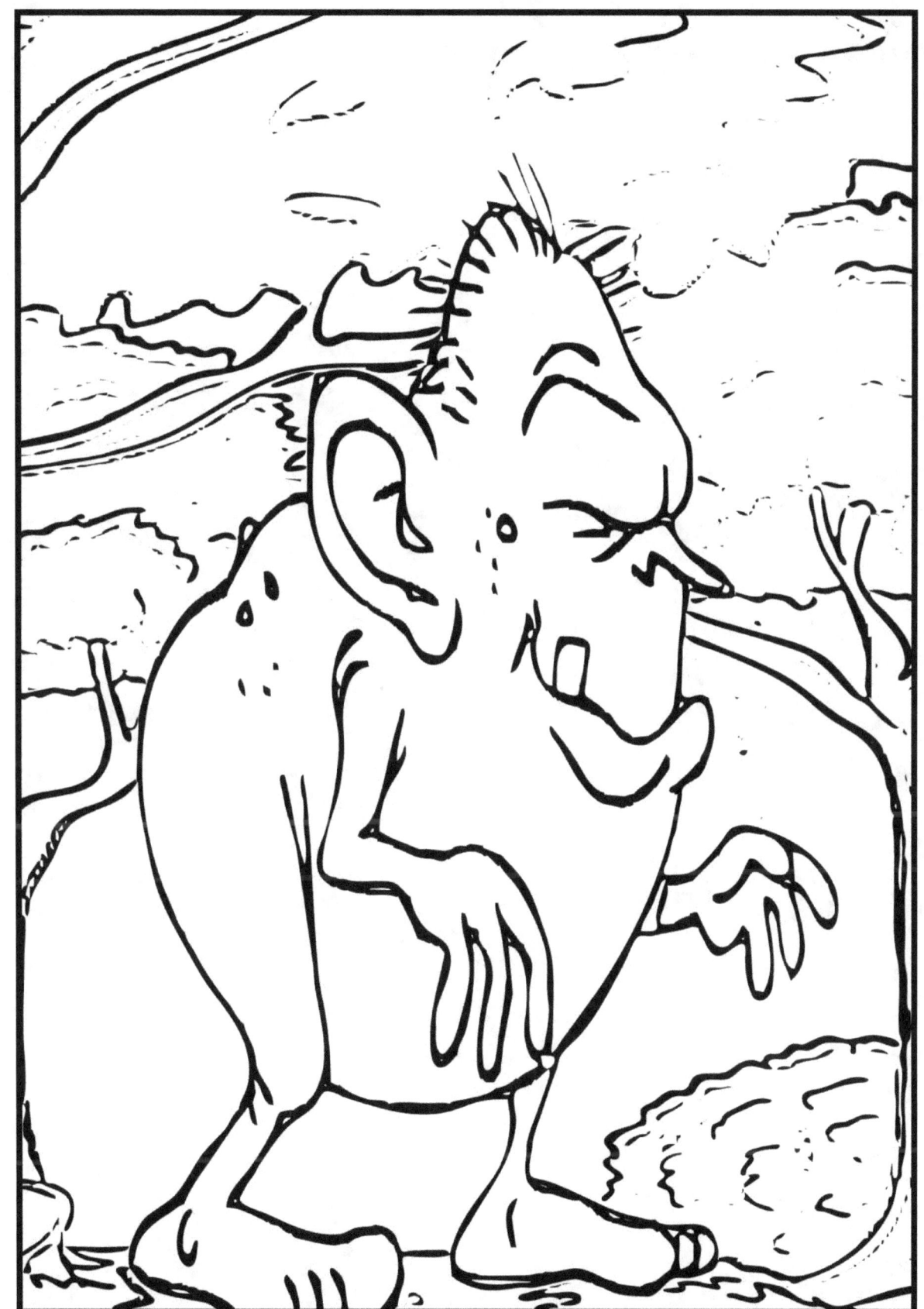

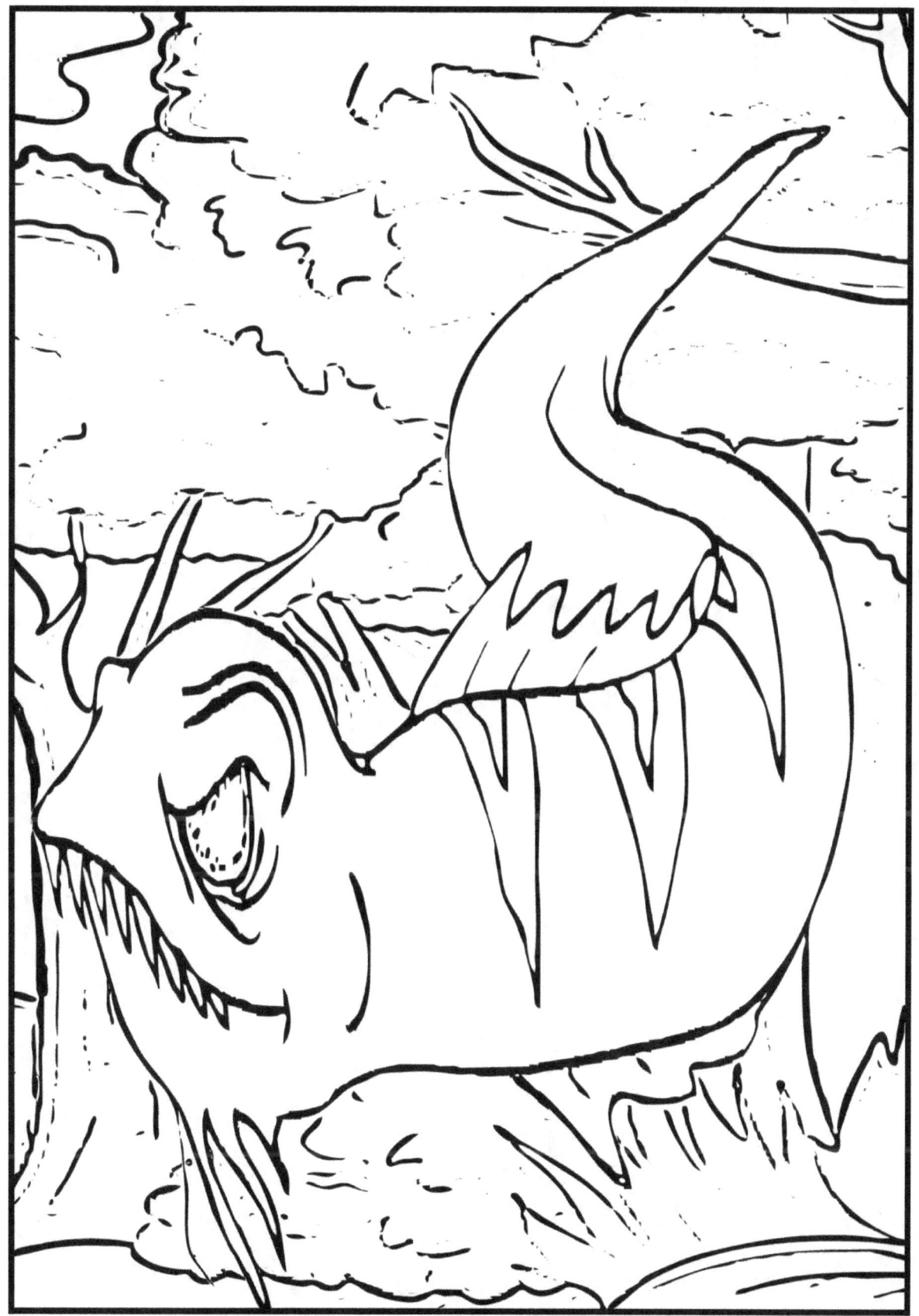

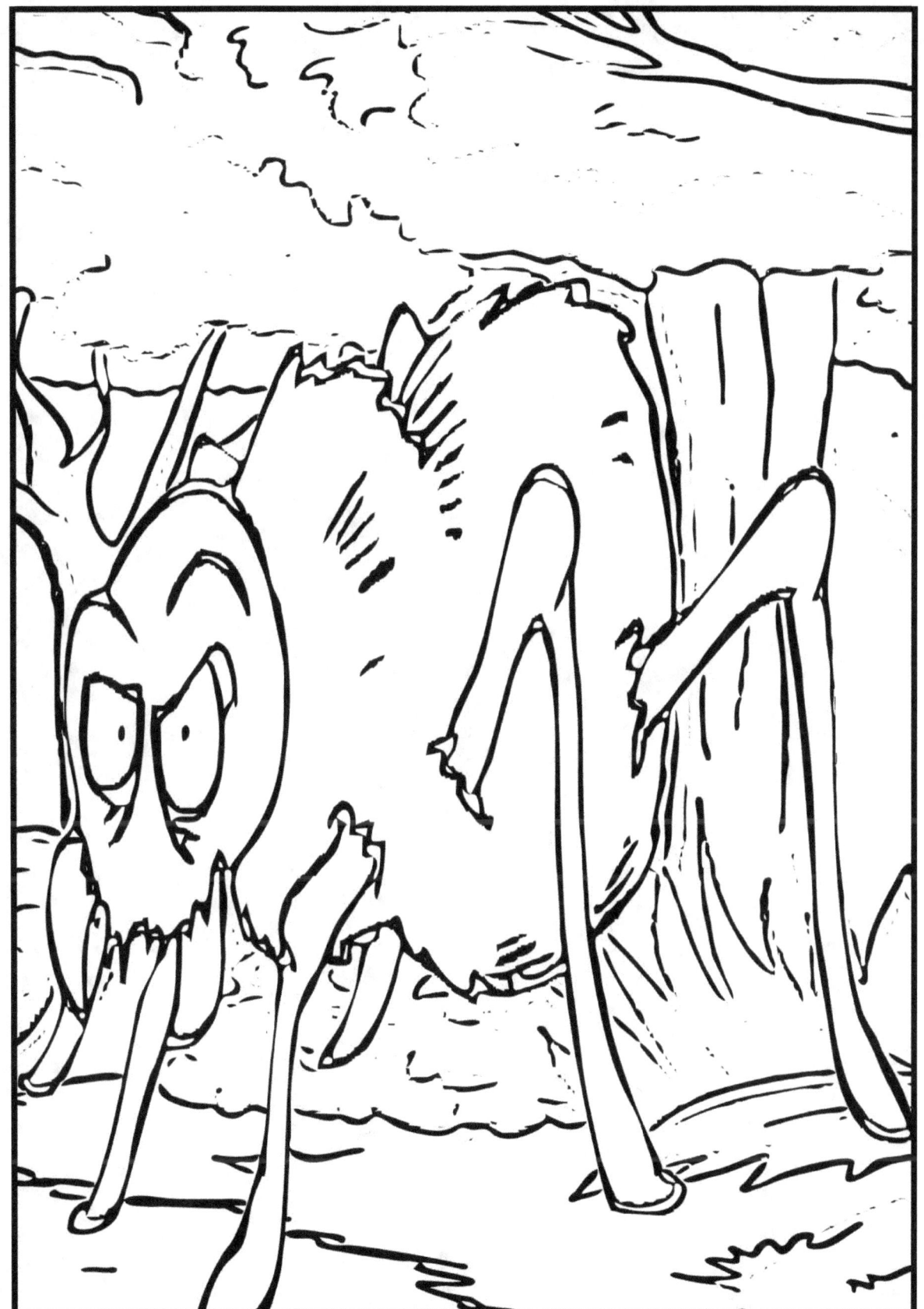

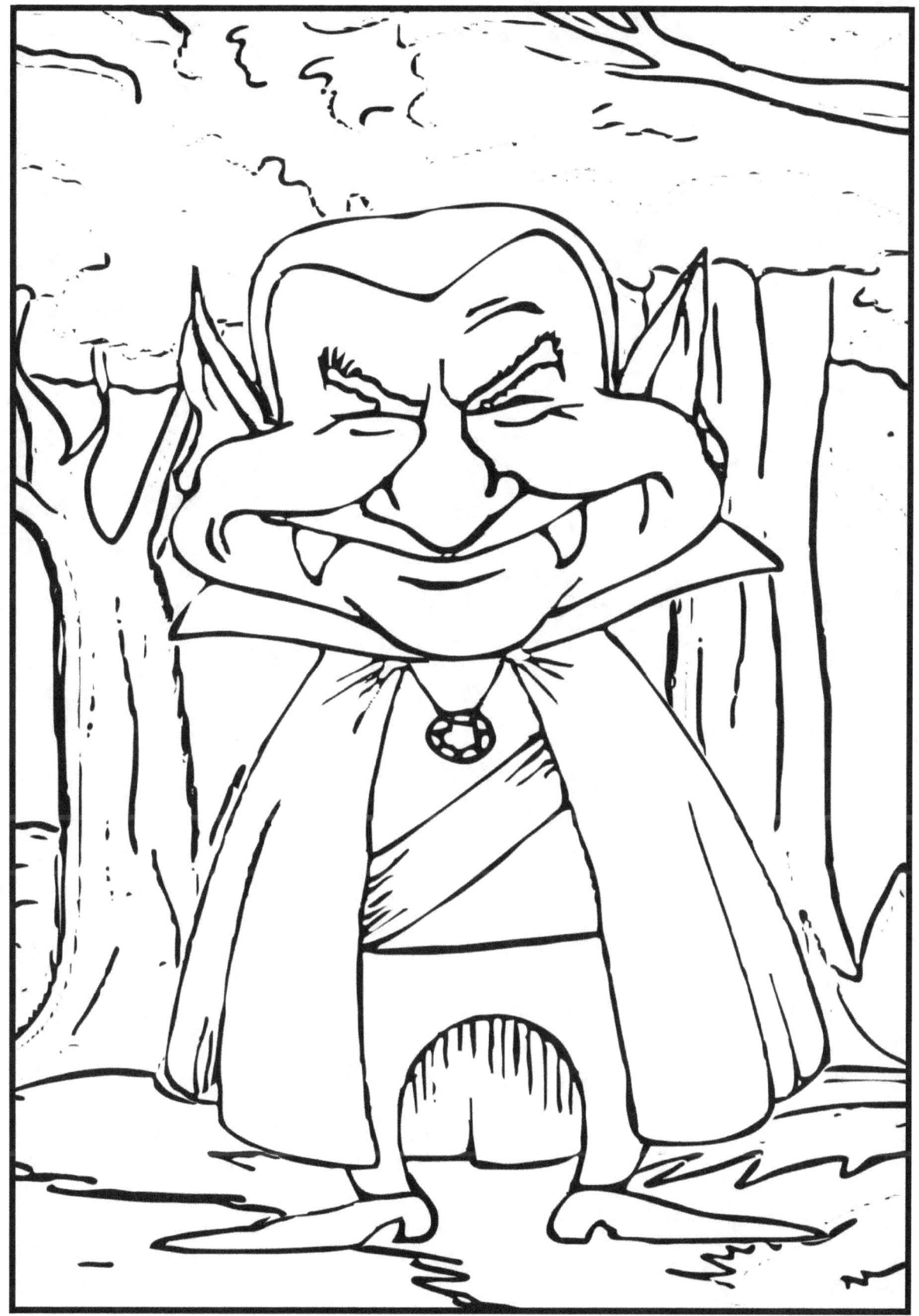

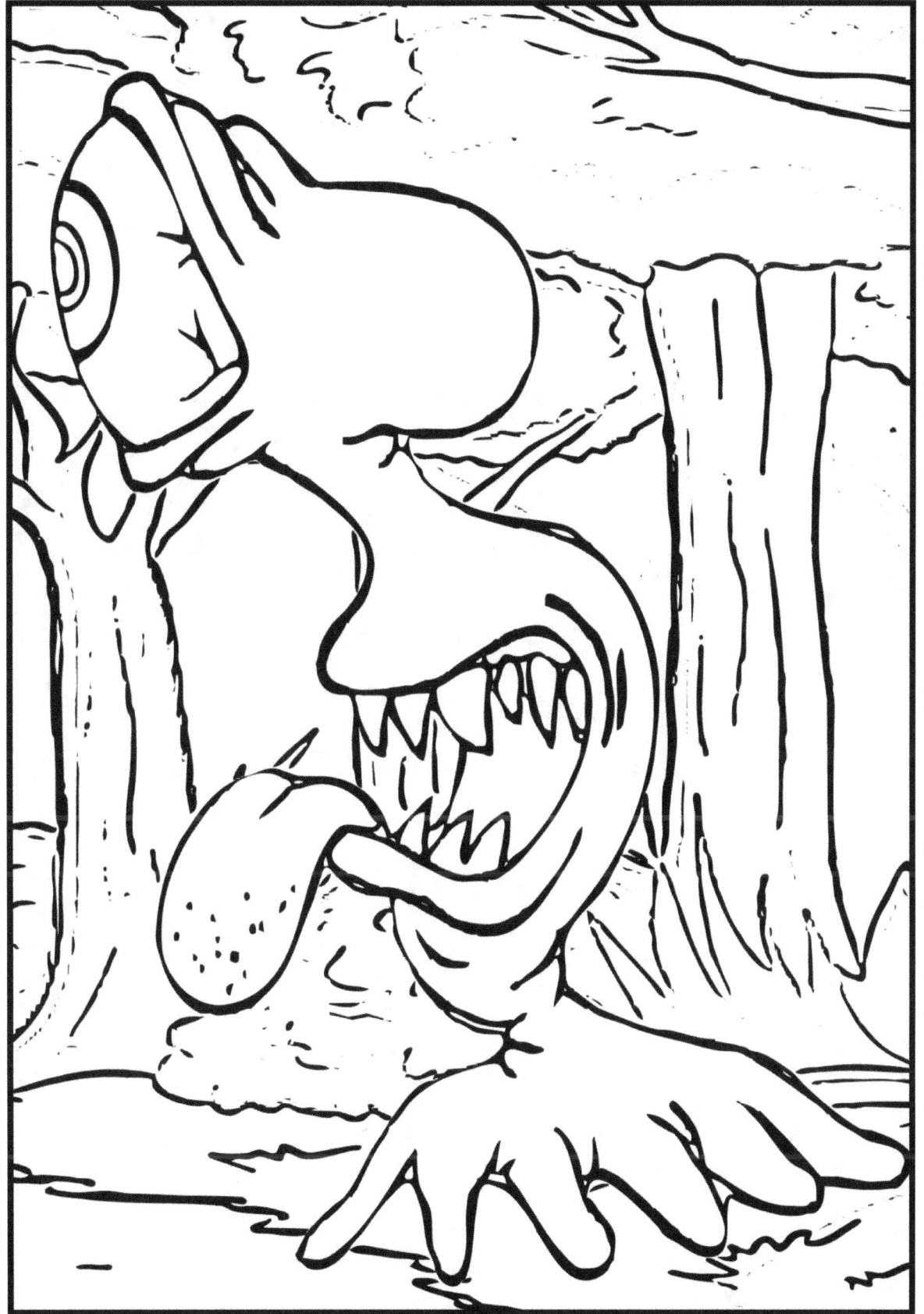

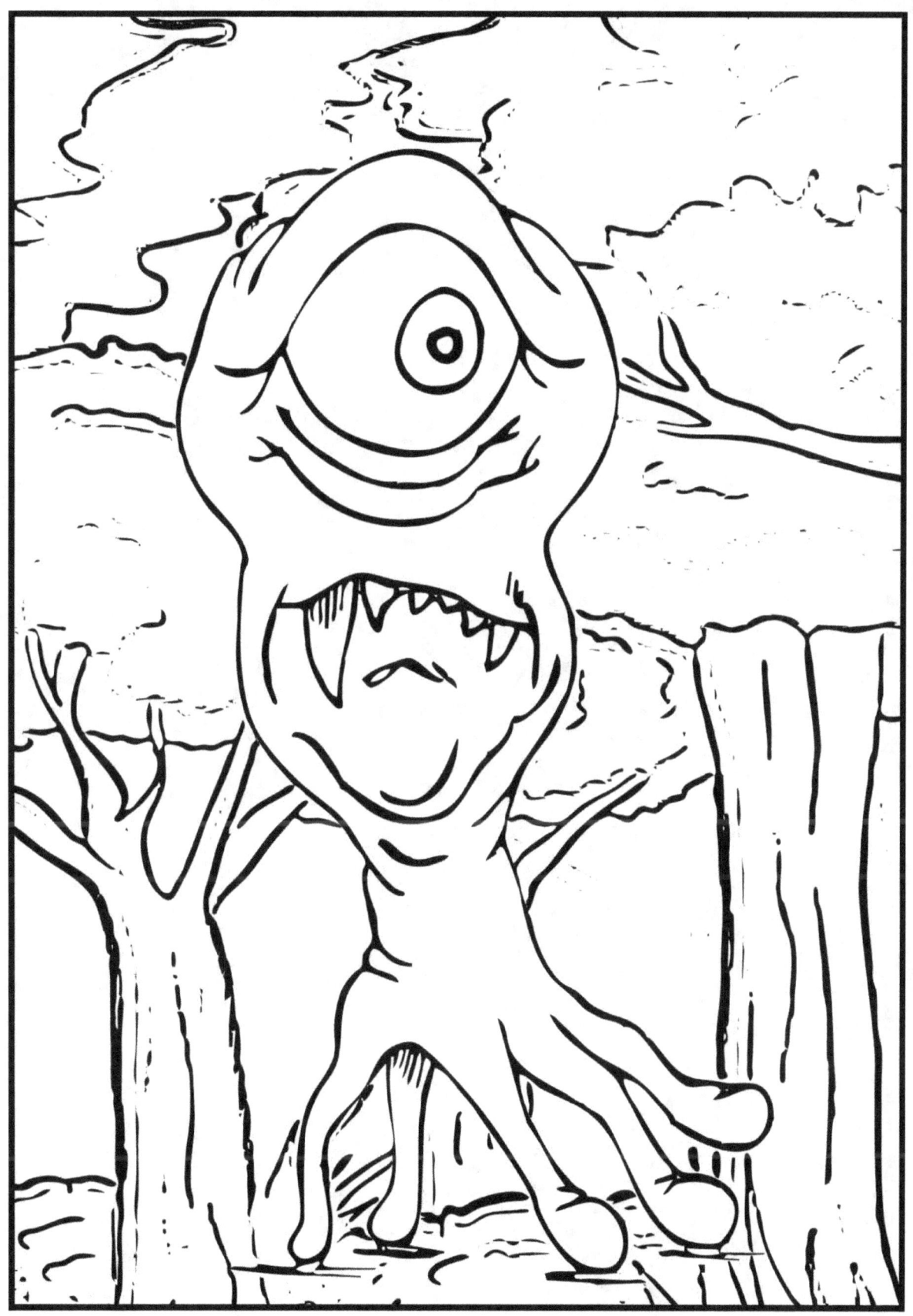

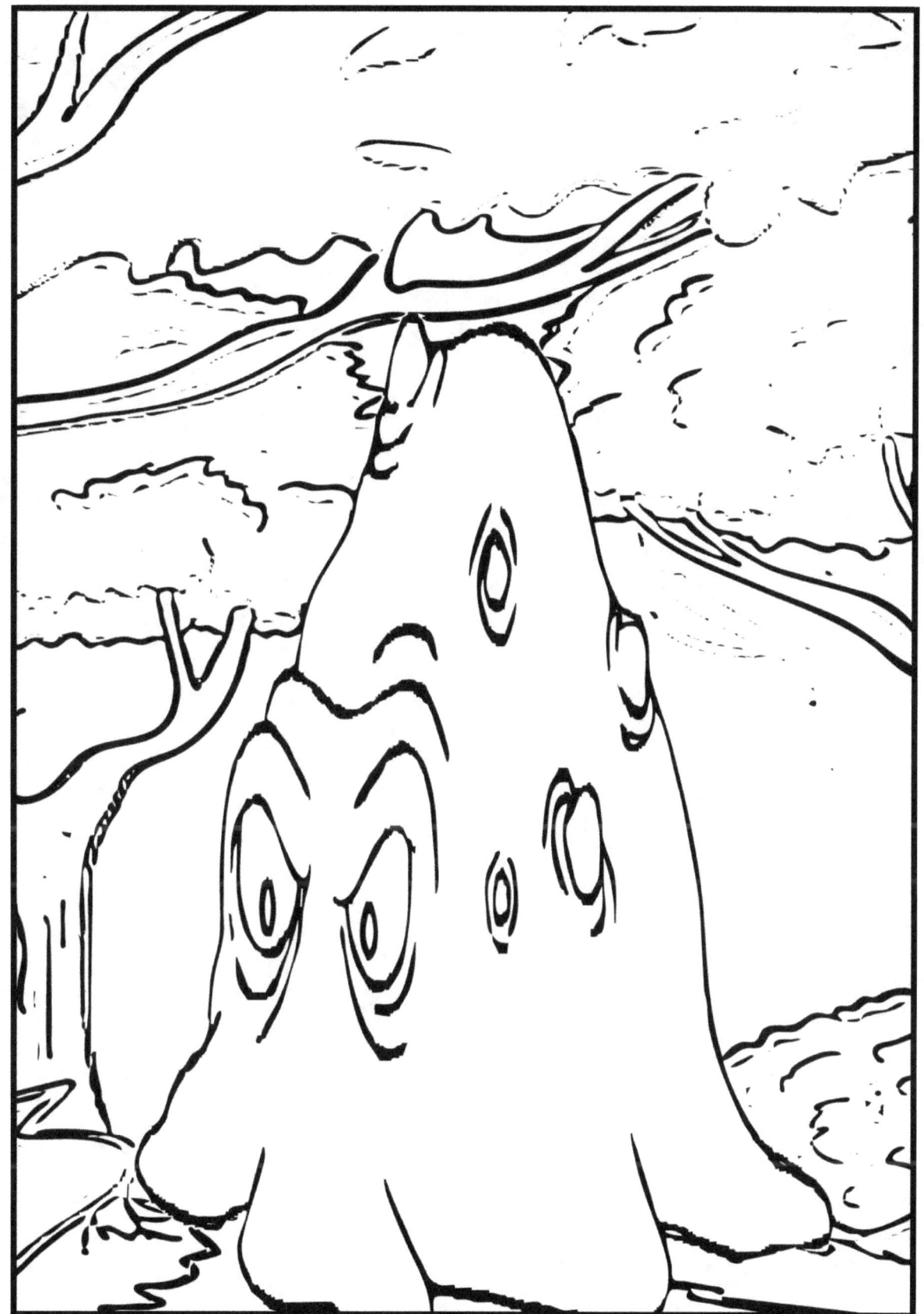

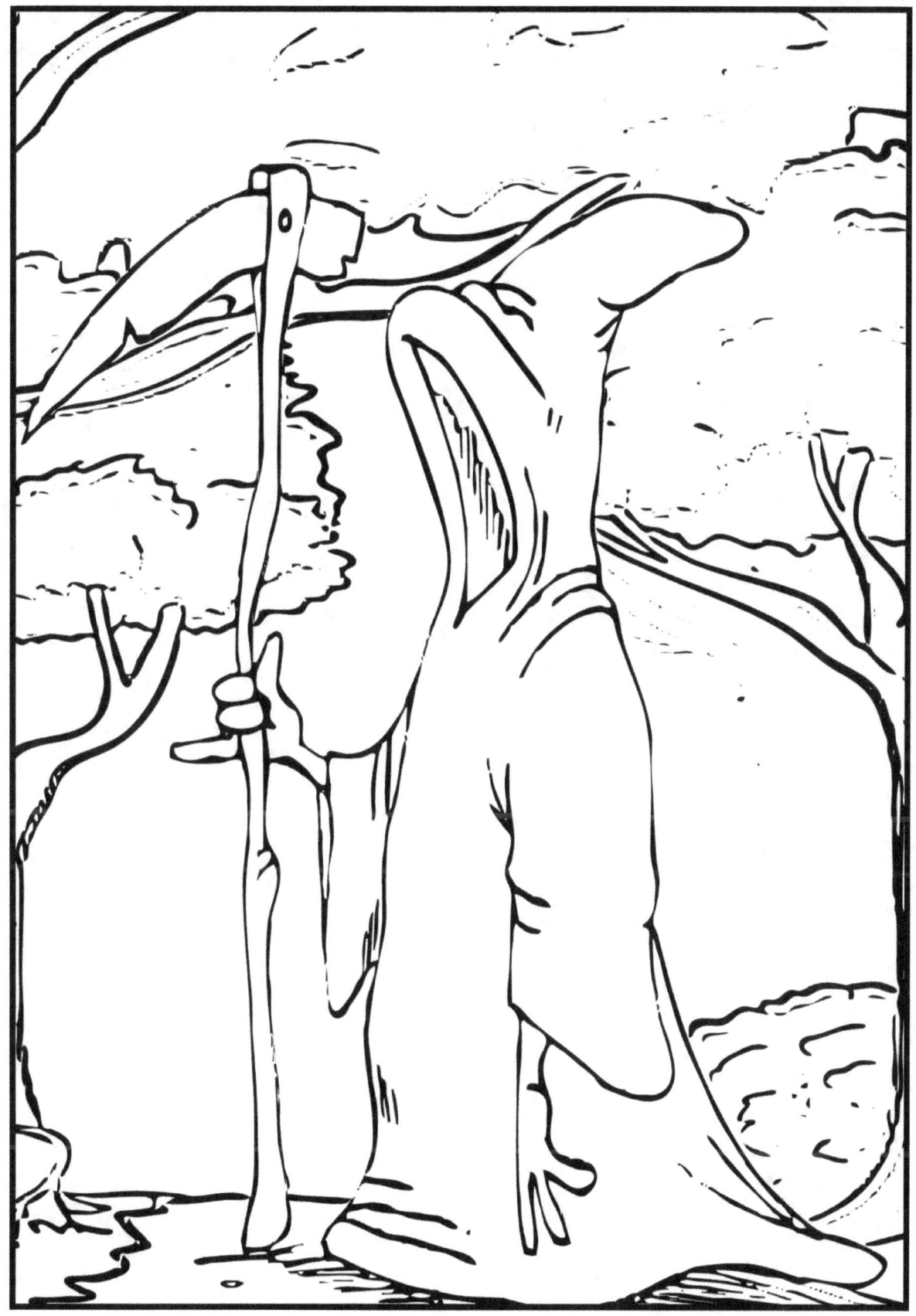

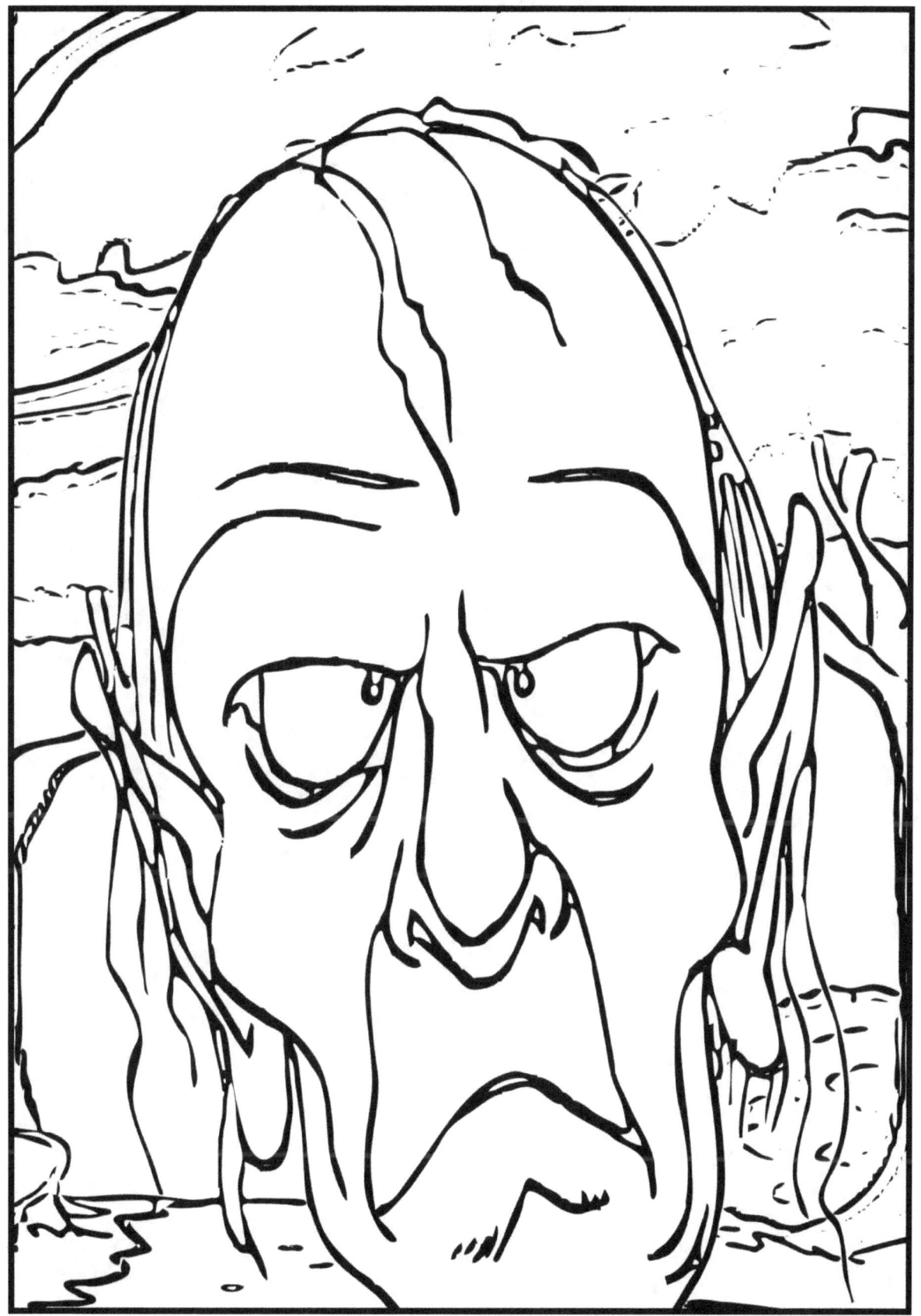

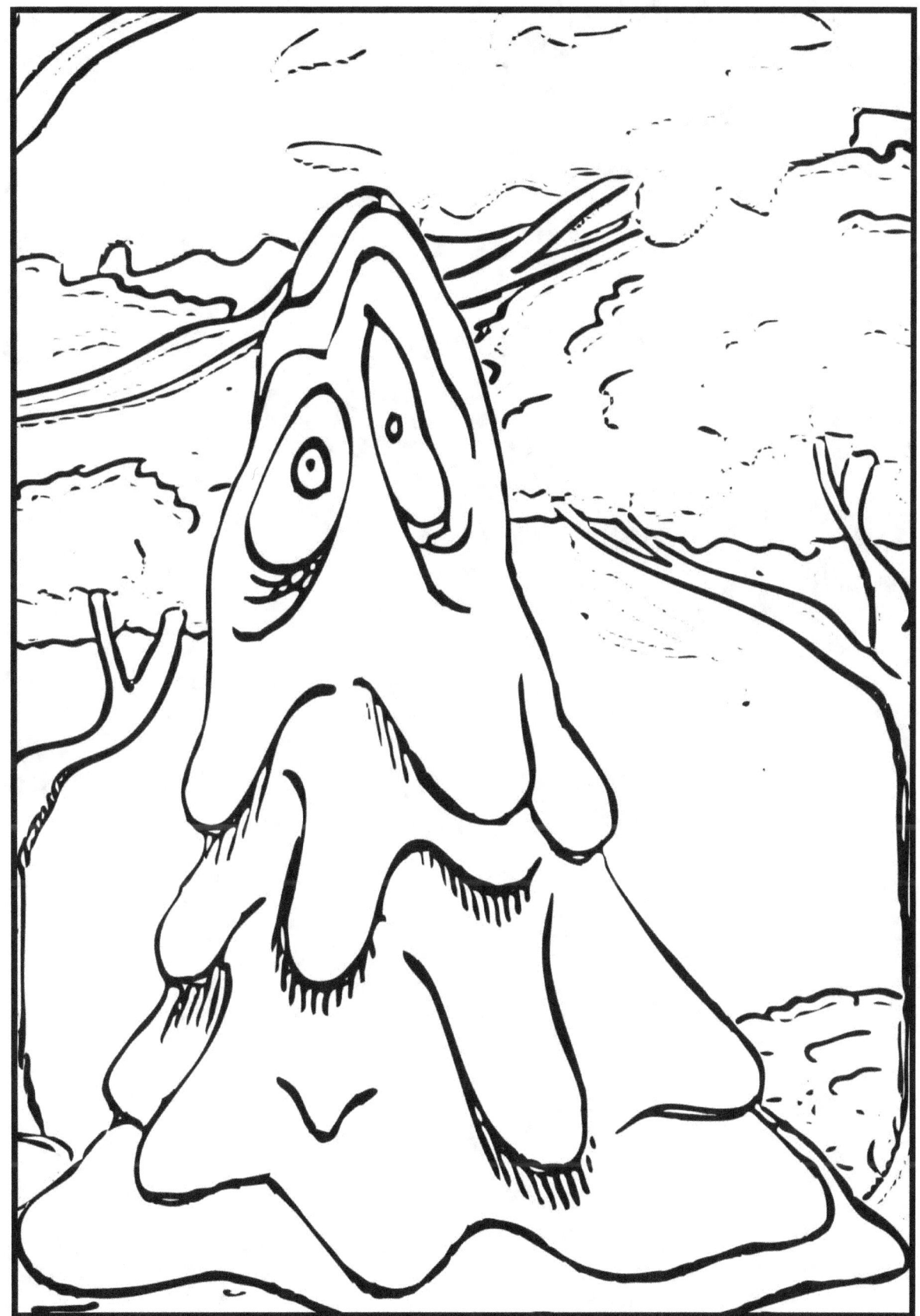

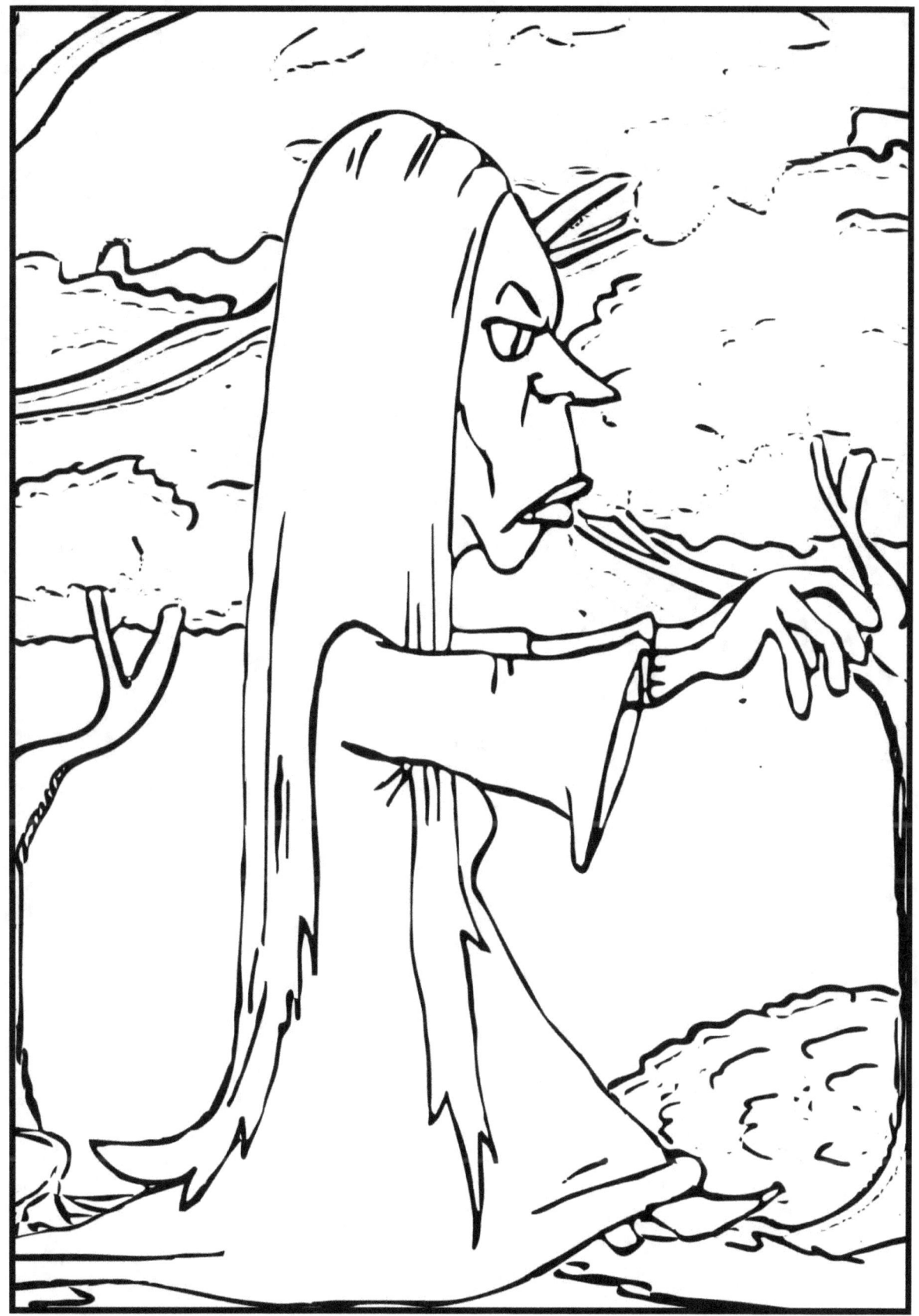

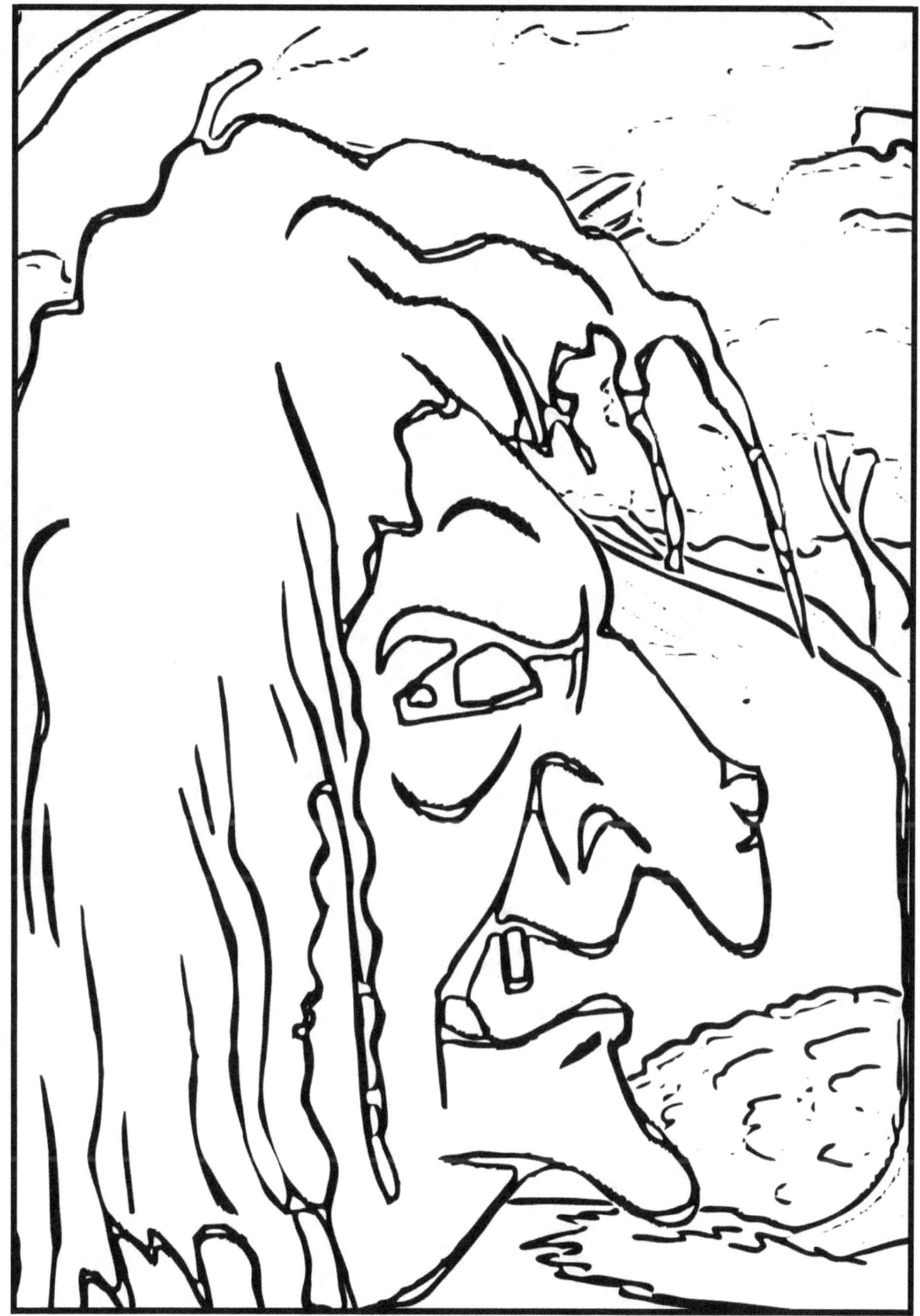

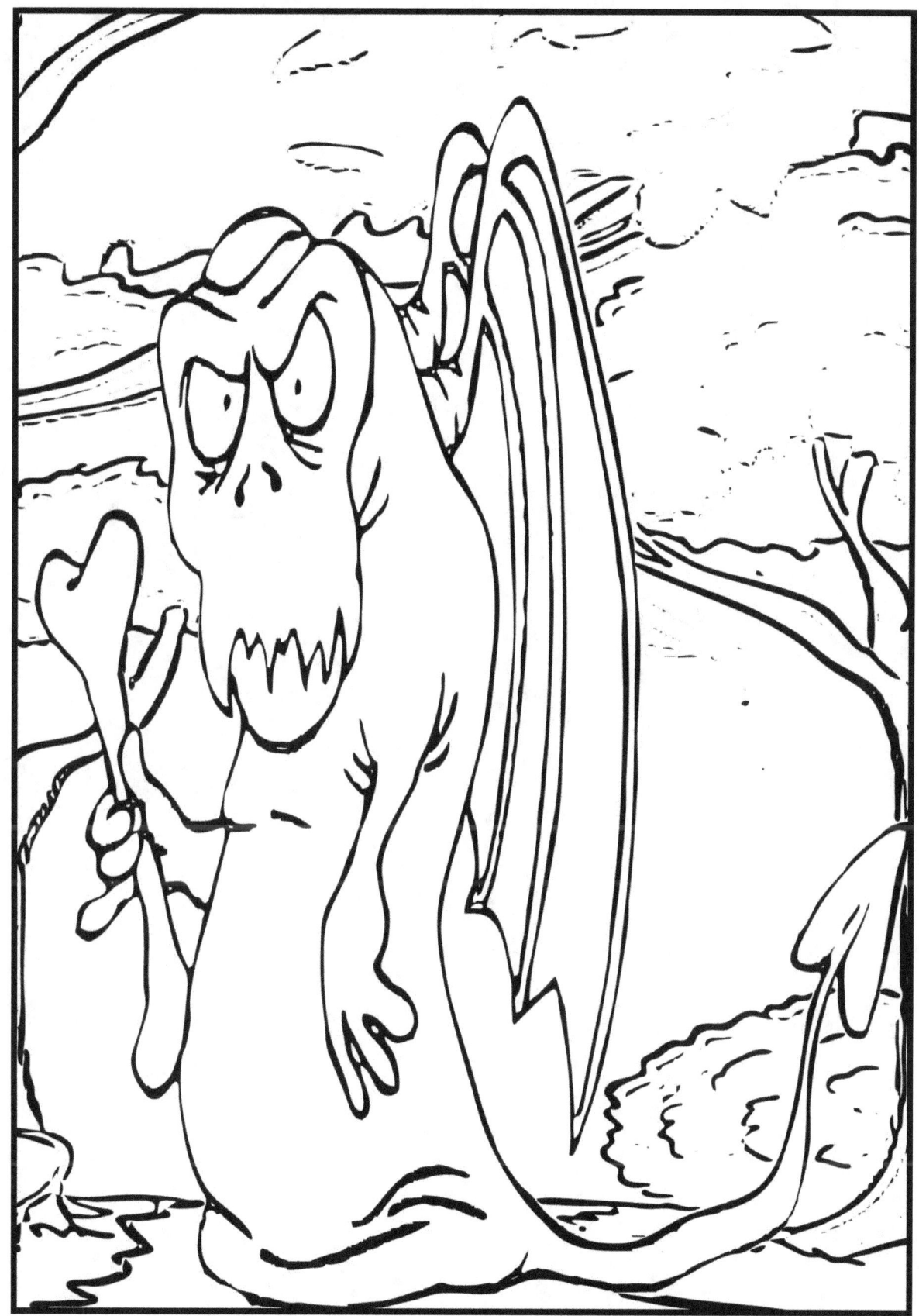

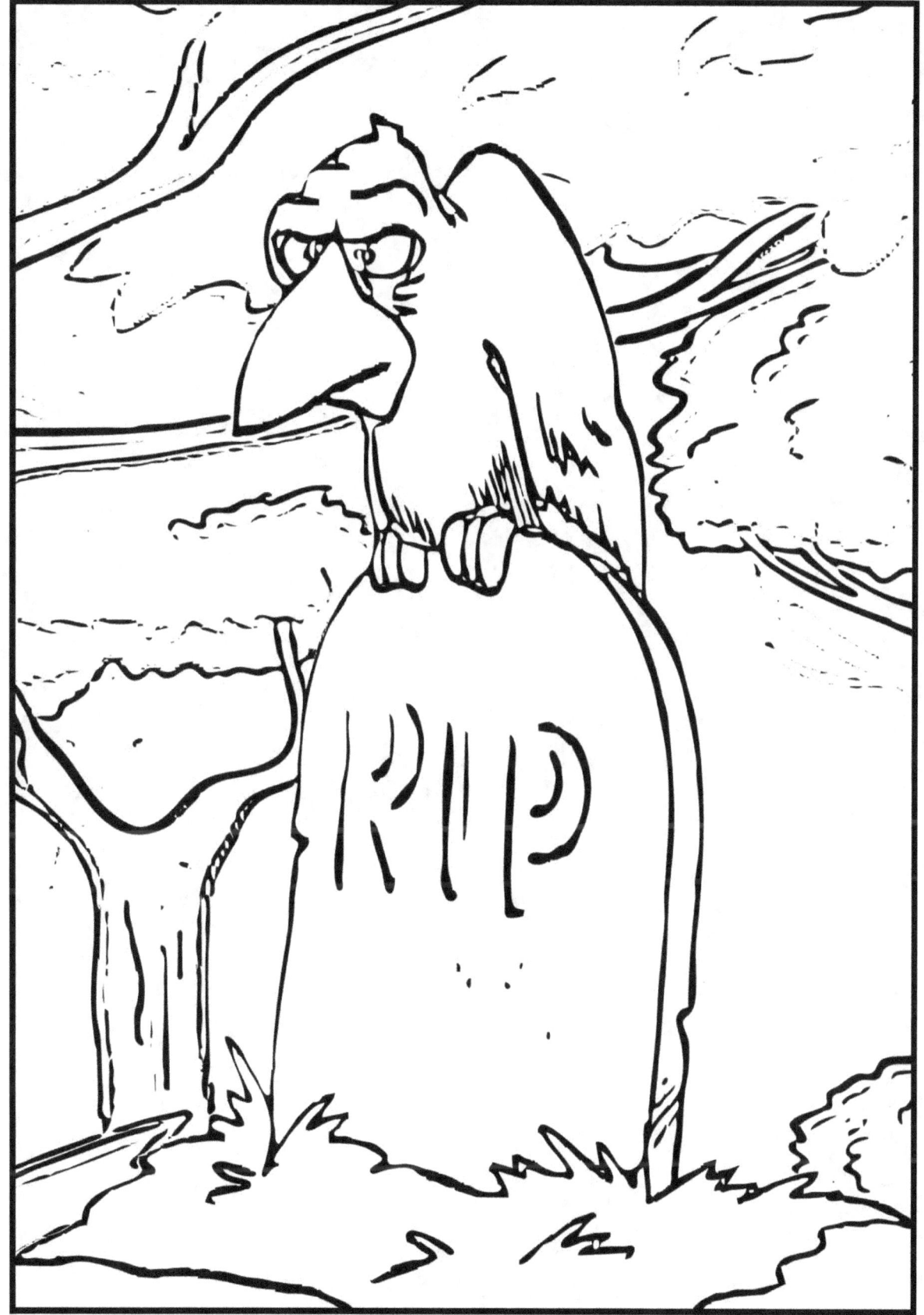

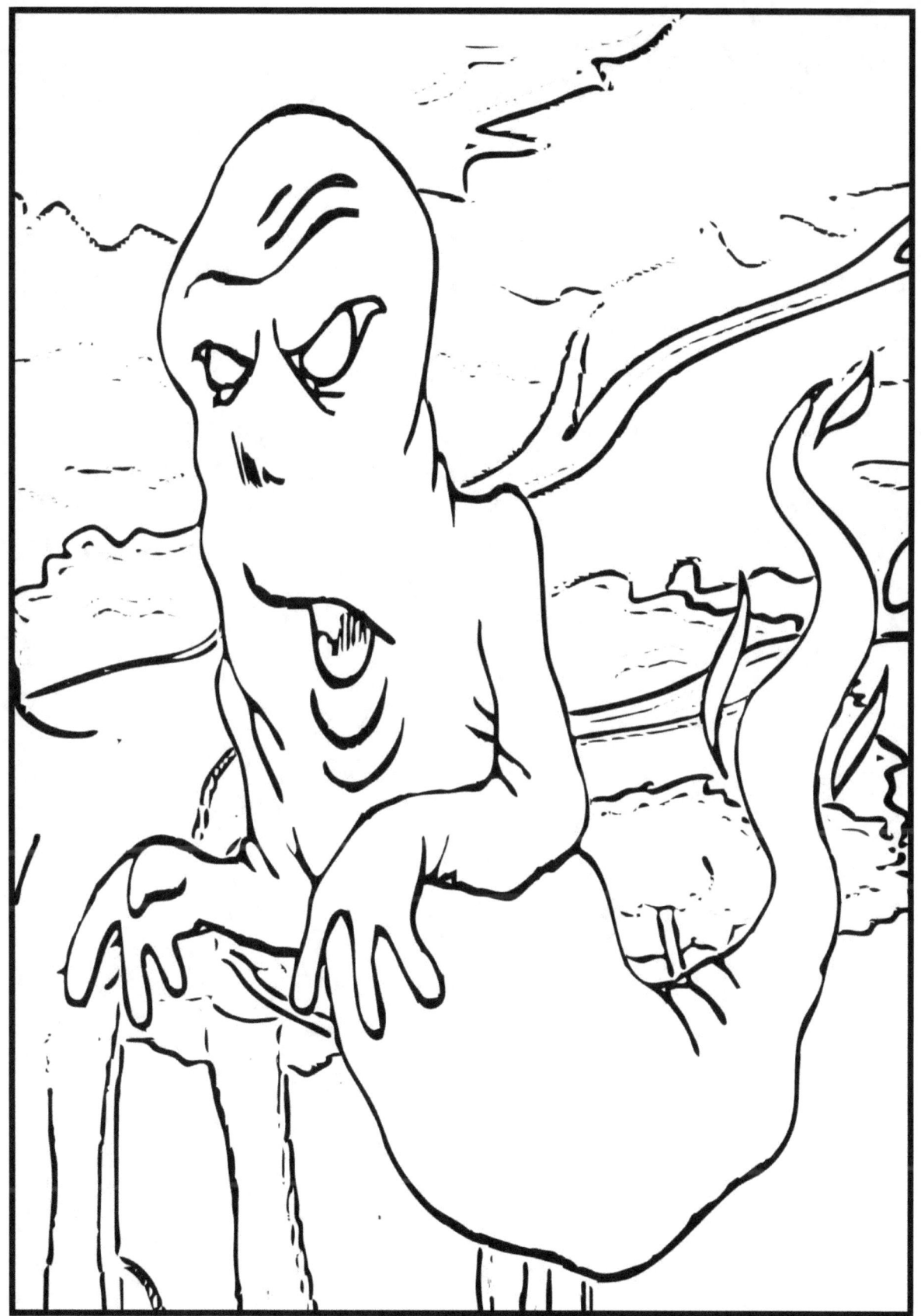

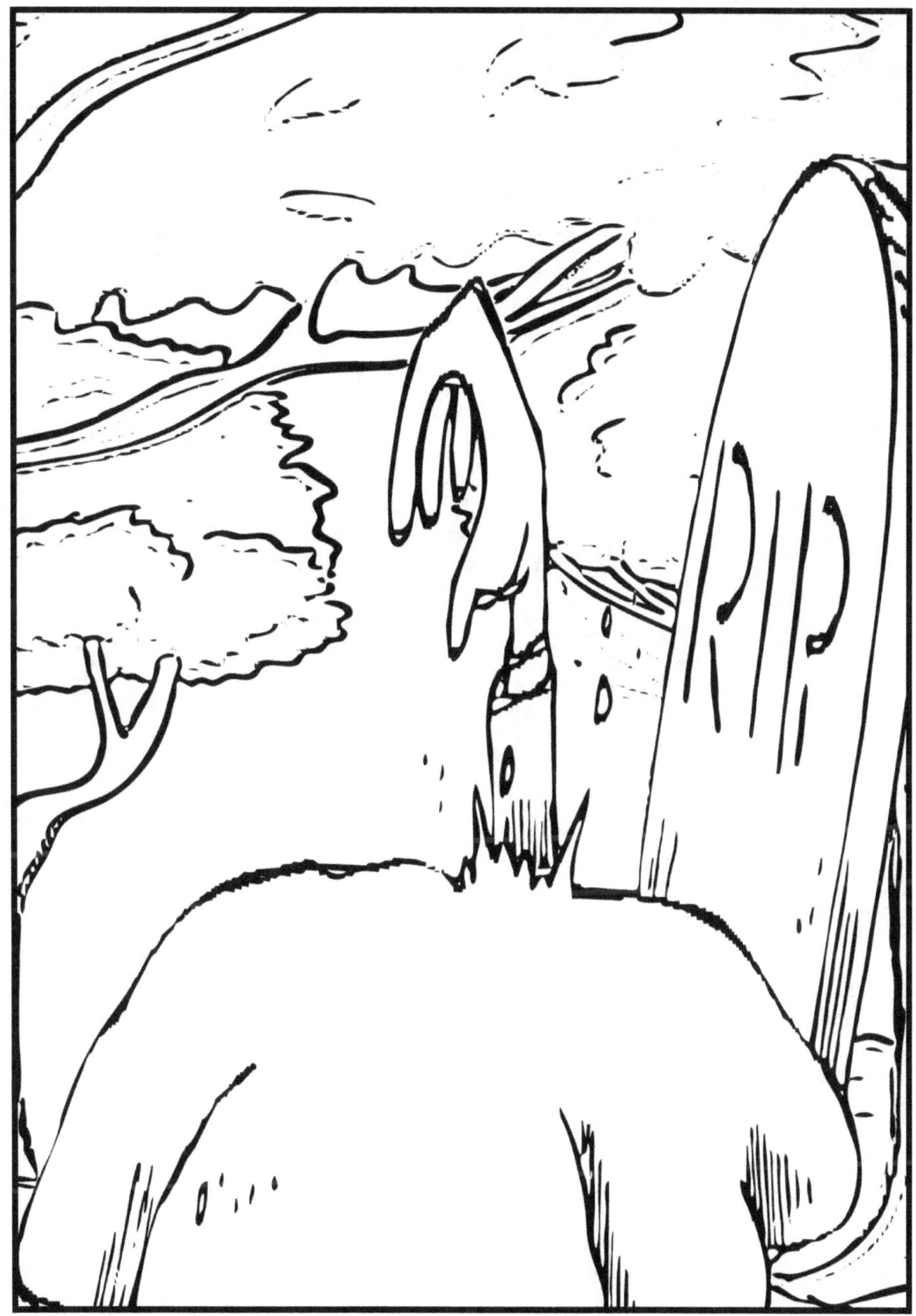

Horror Coloring Book For Adults
CLOWNING AROUND

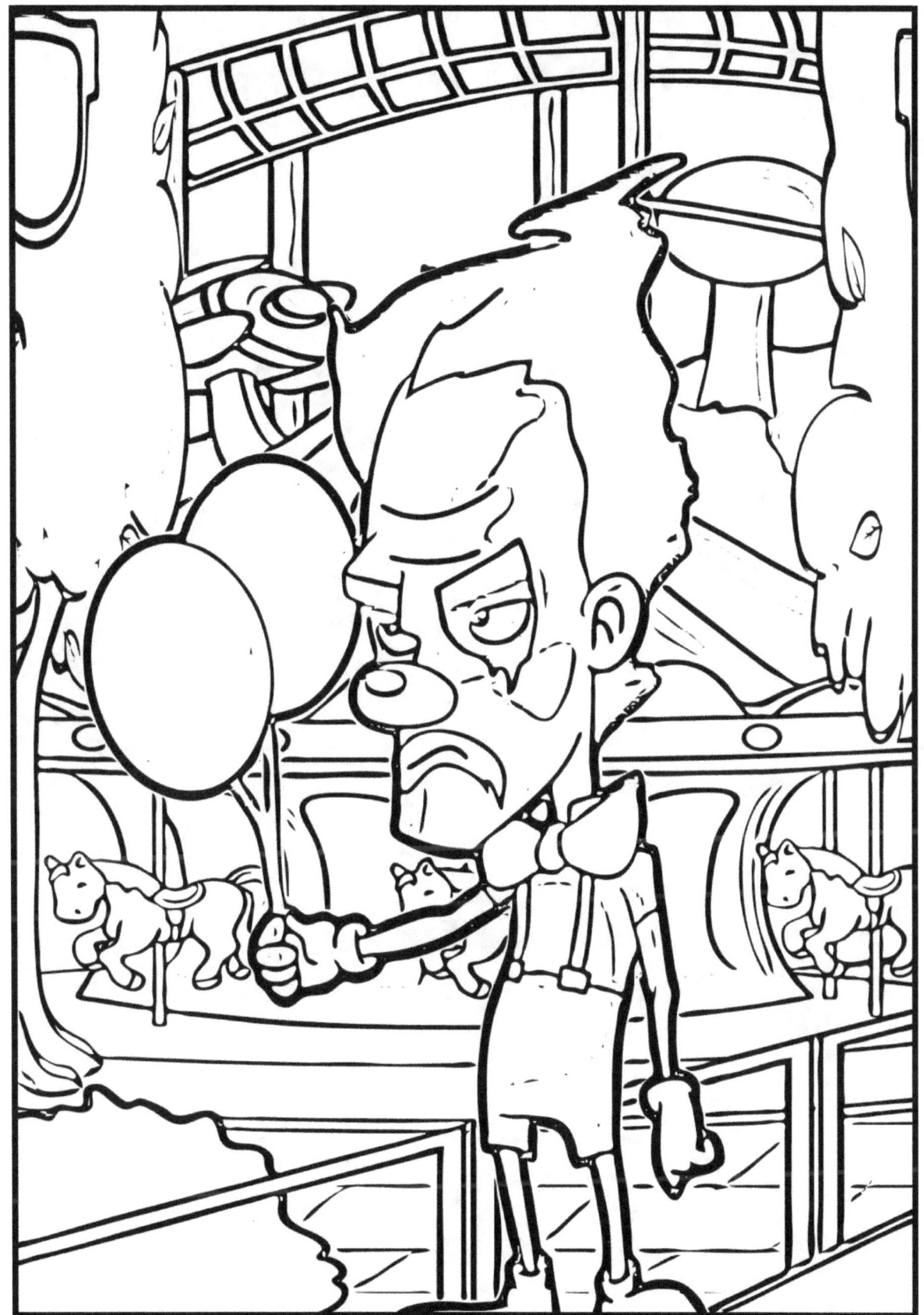

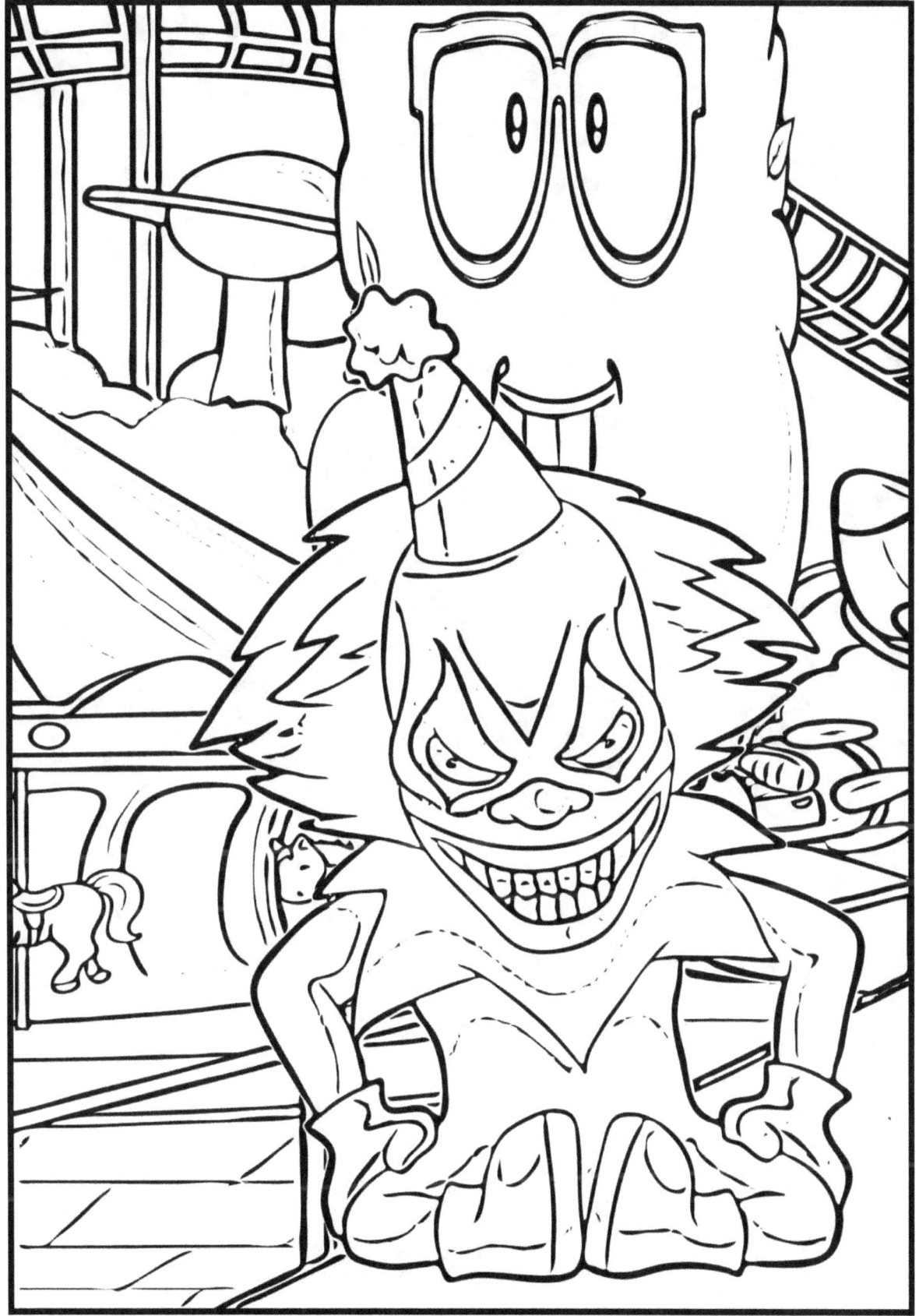

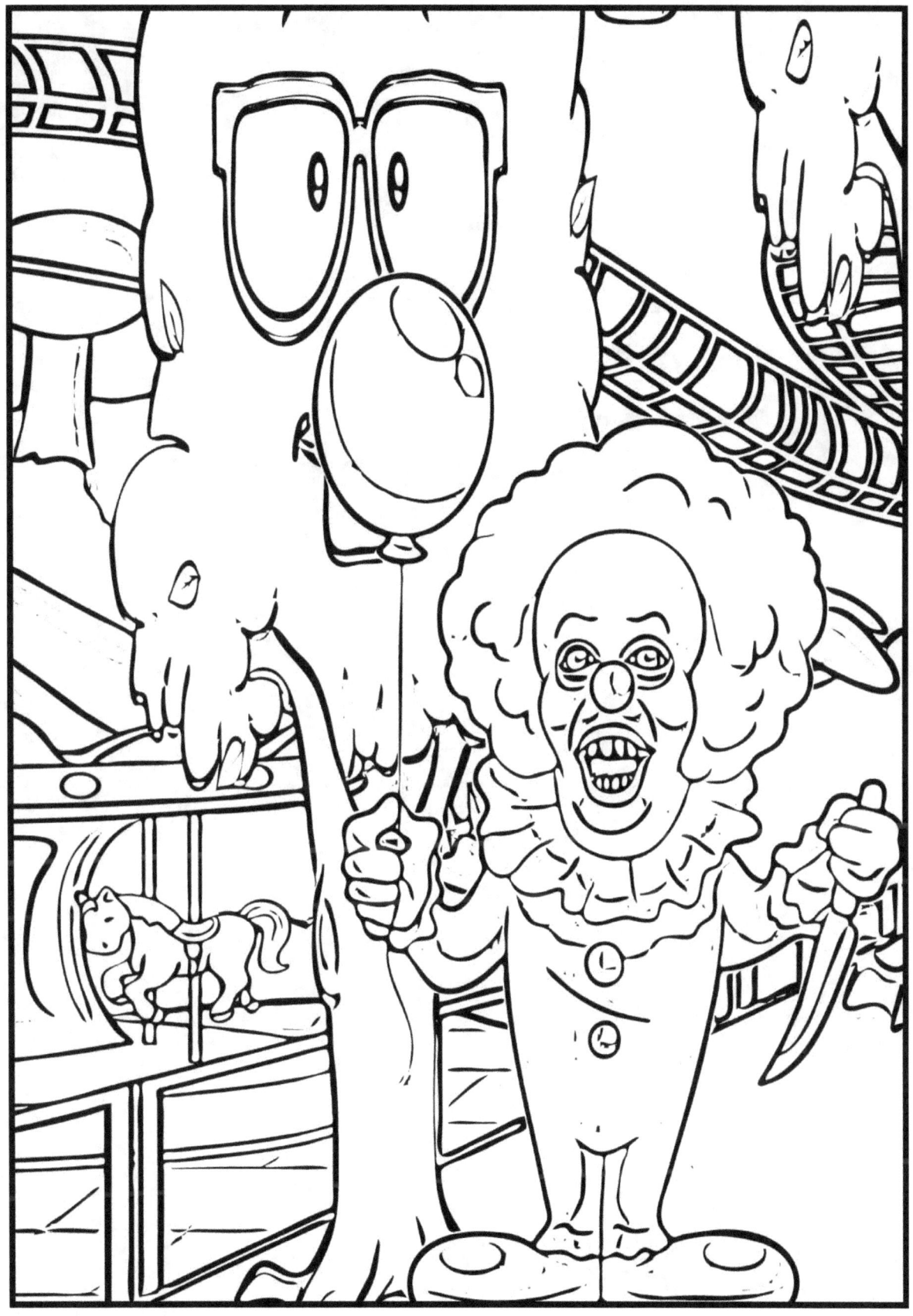

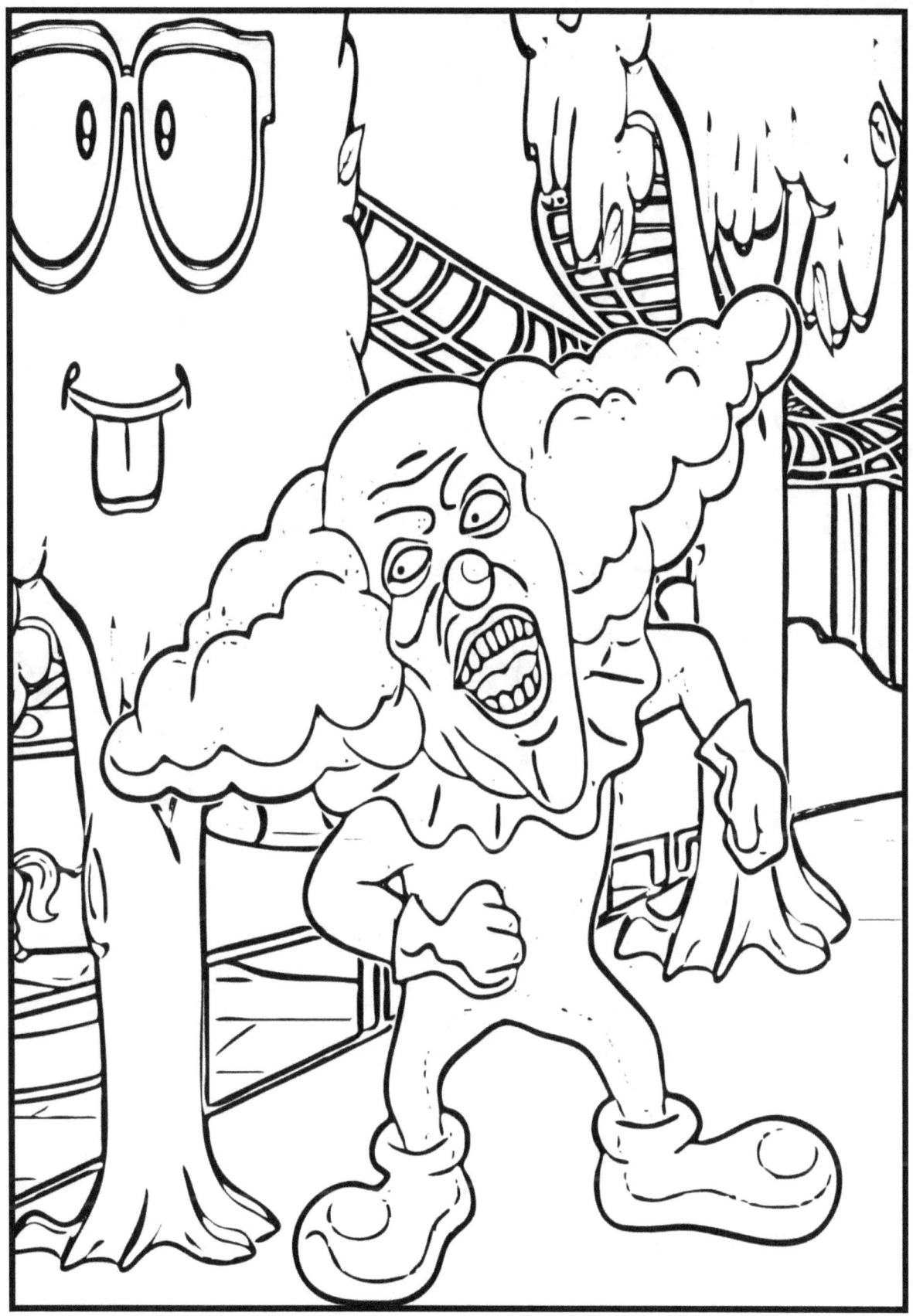

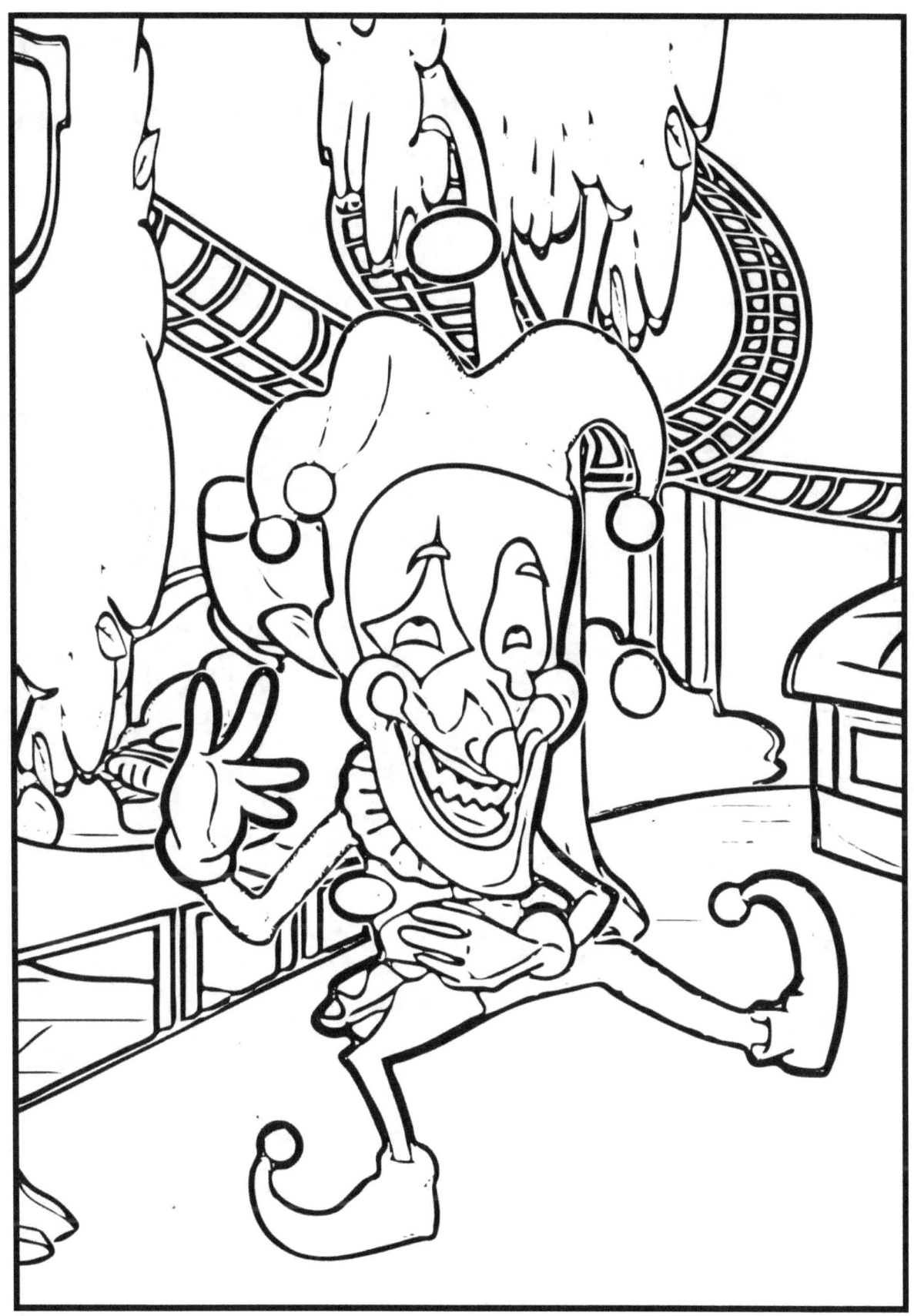

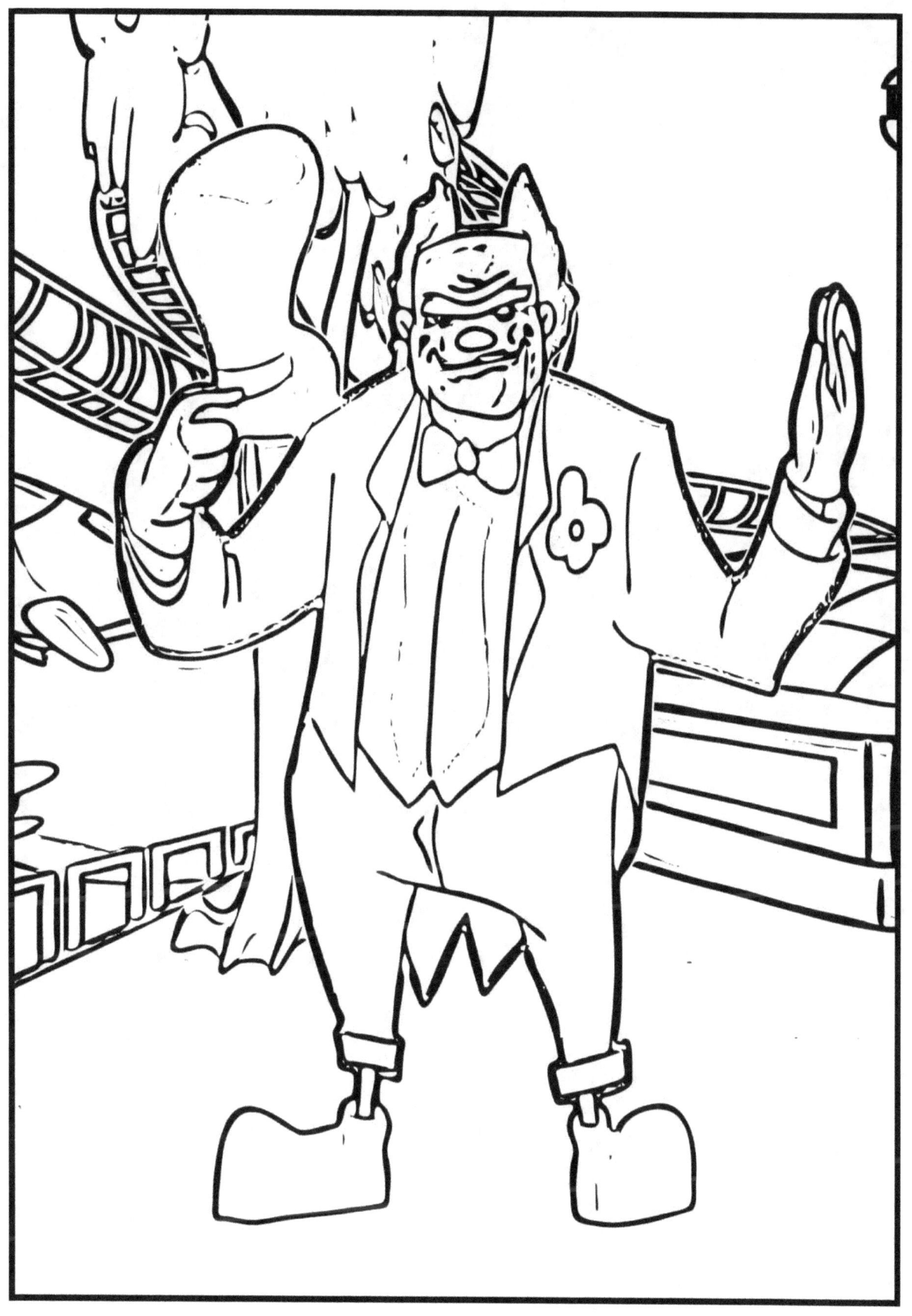

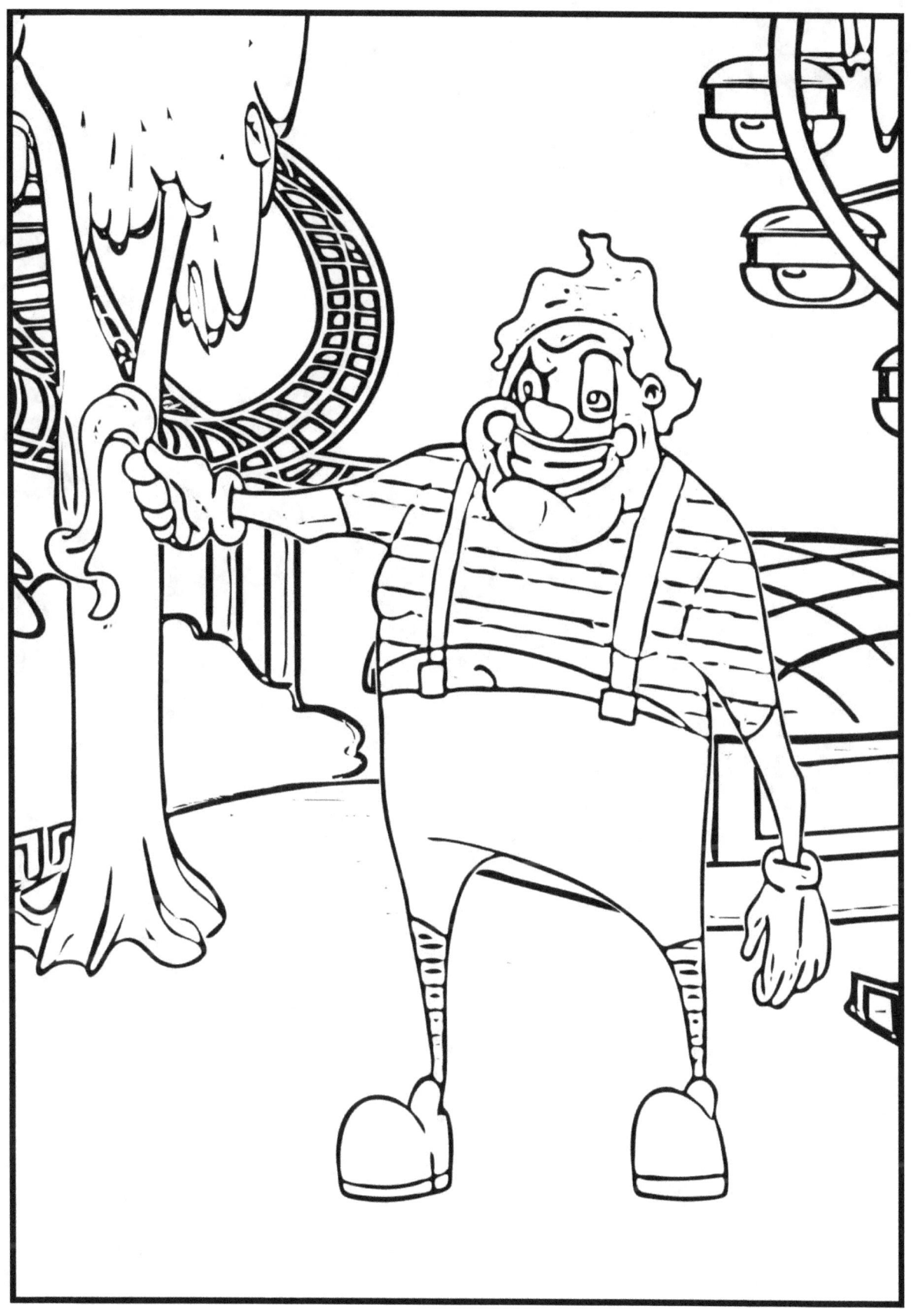

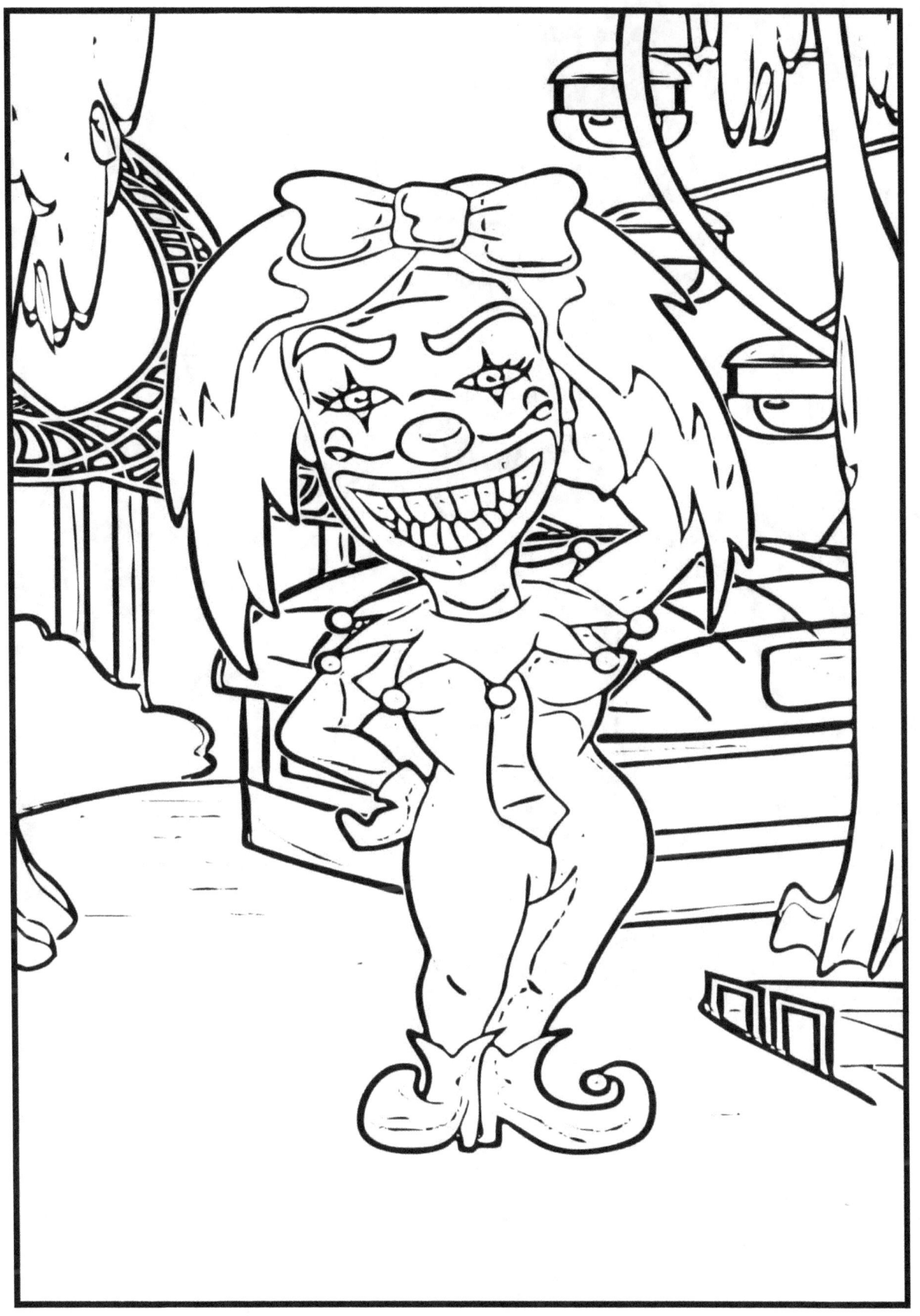

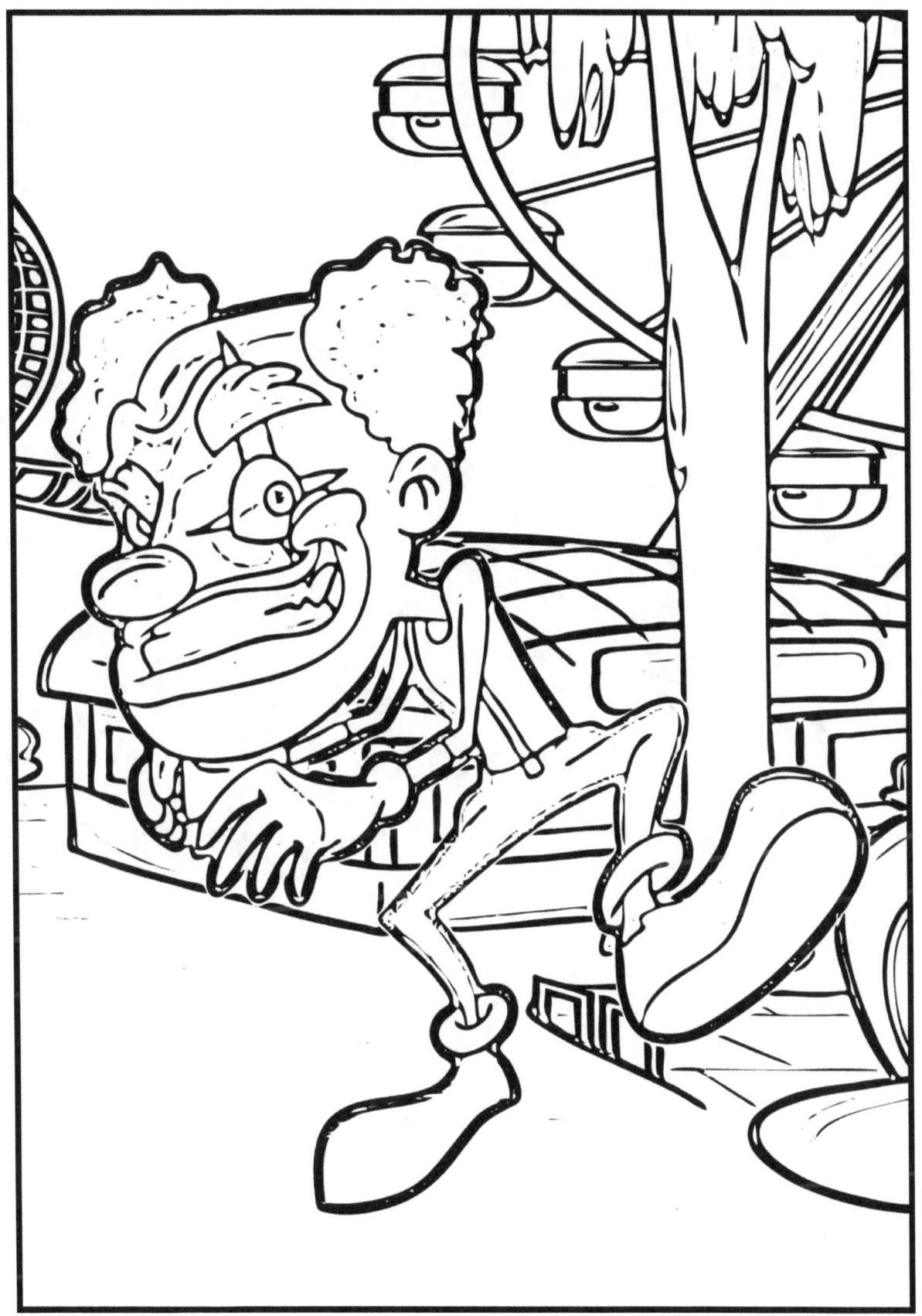

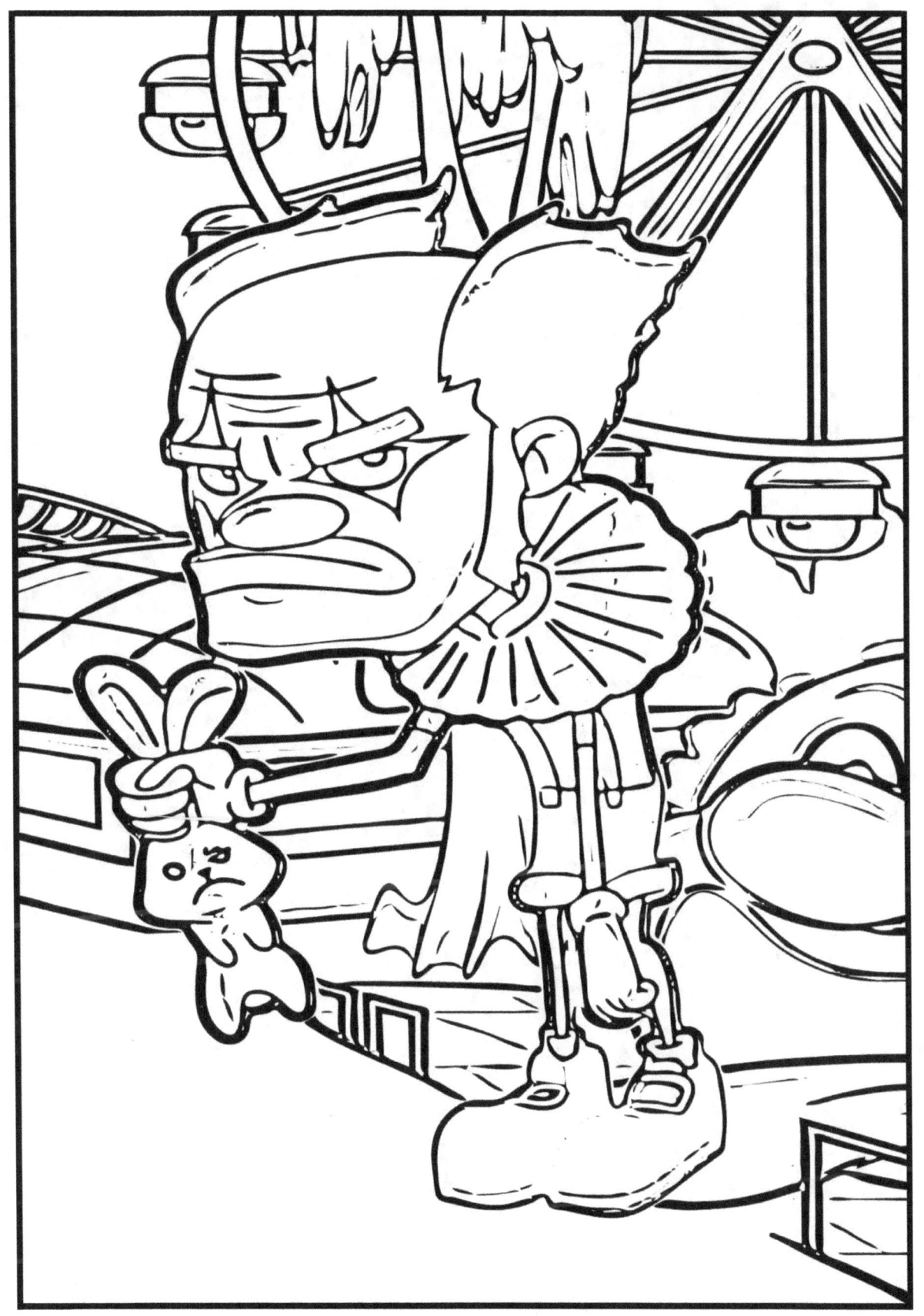

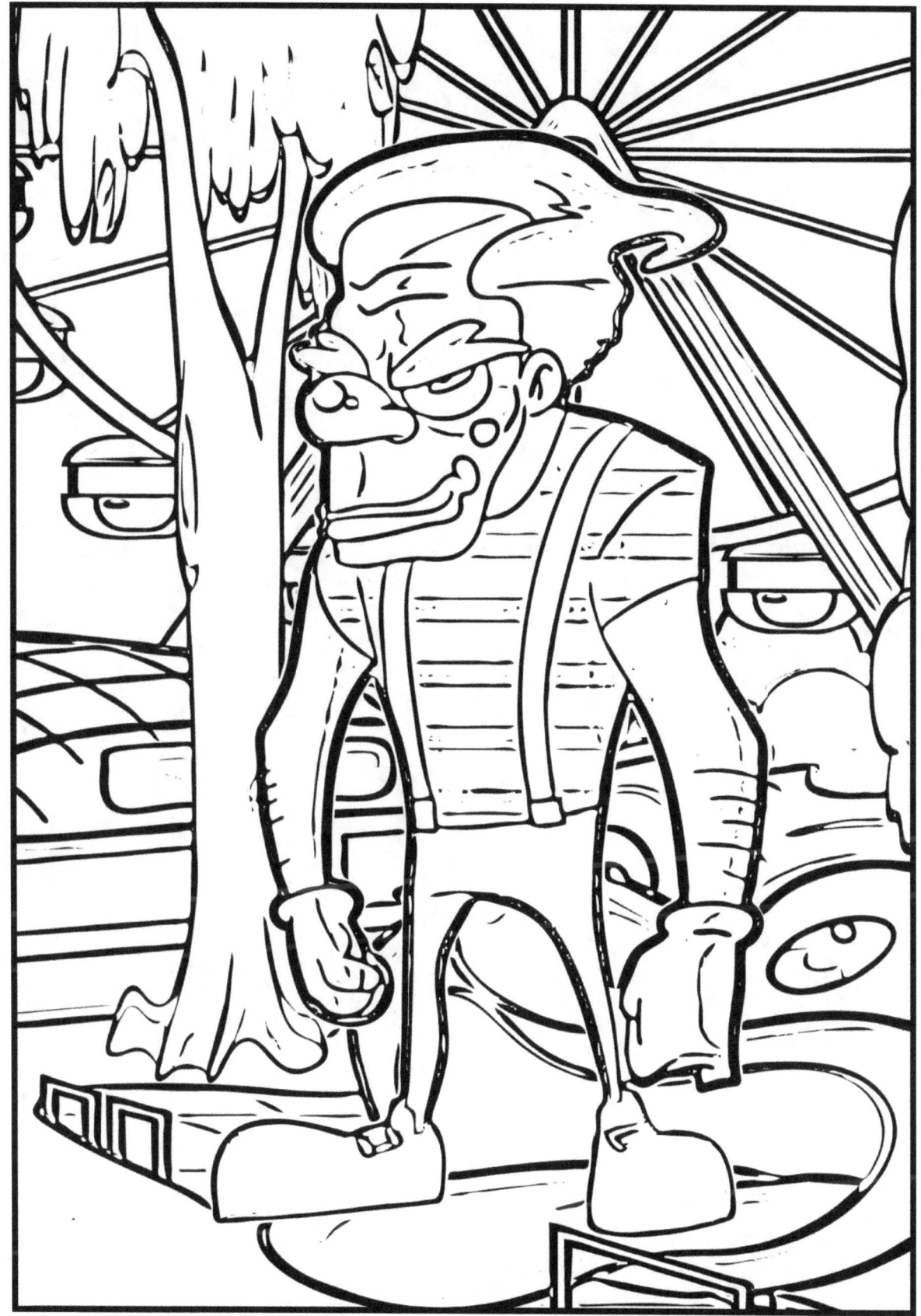

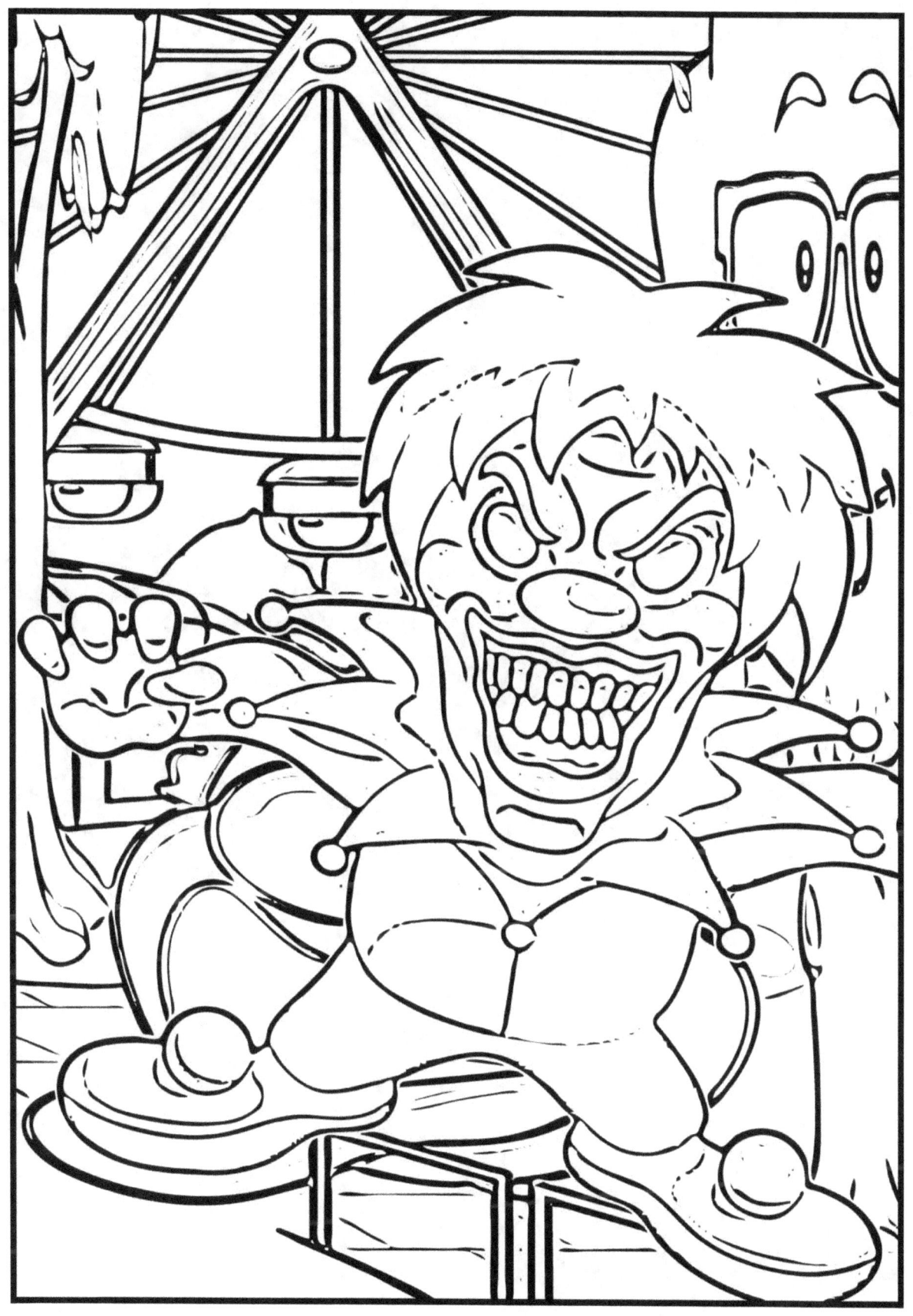

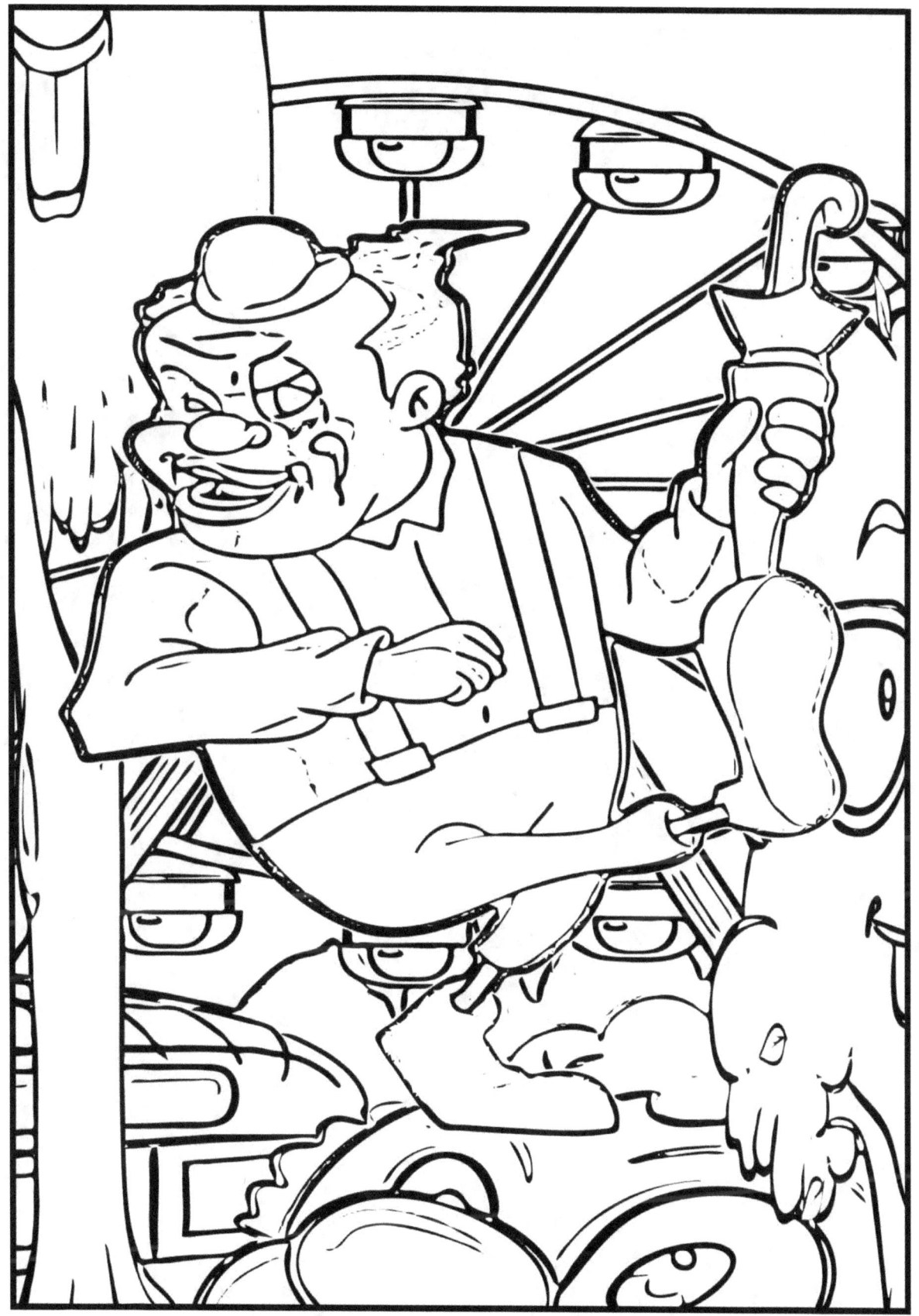

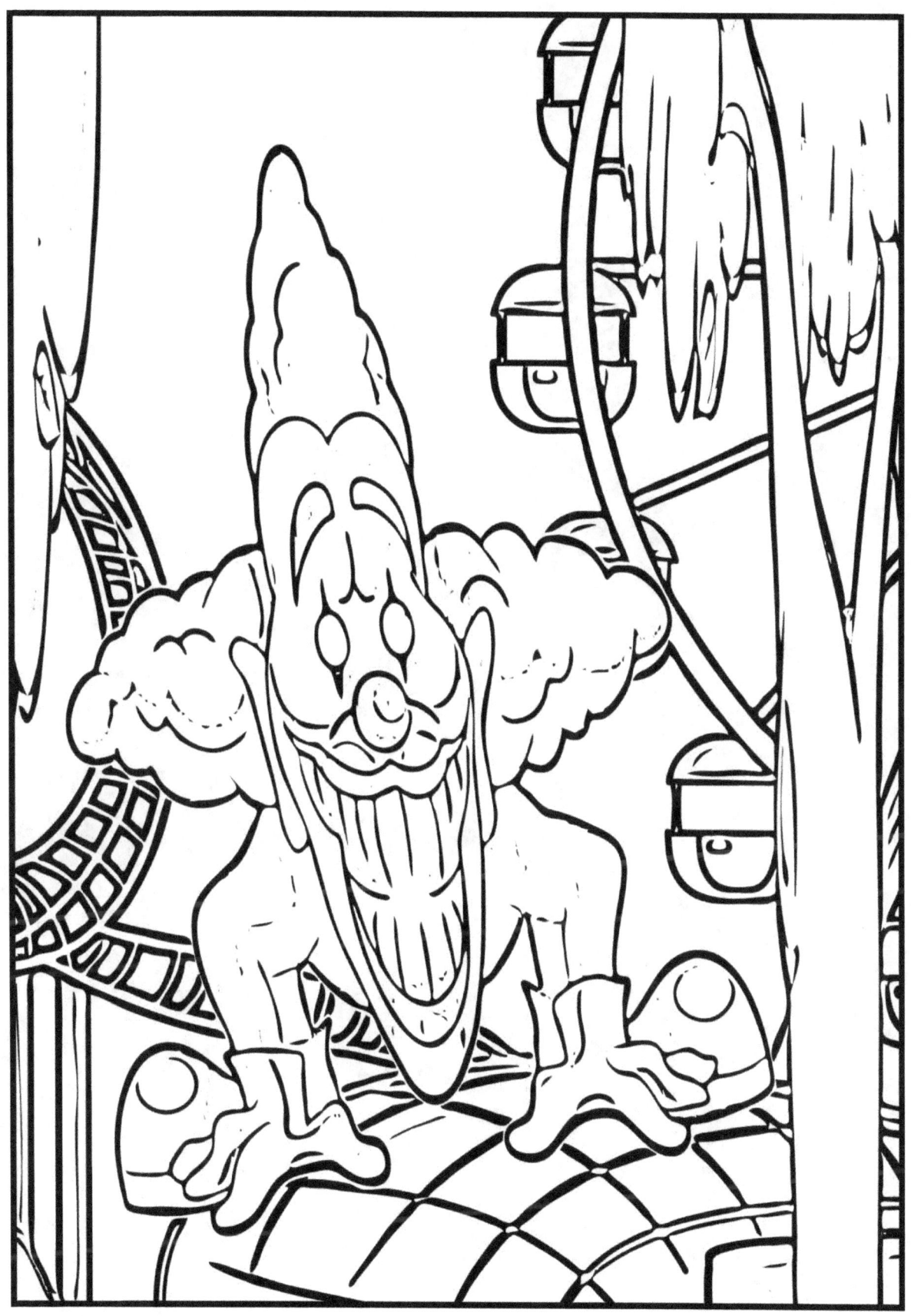

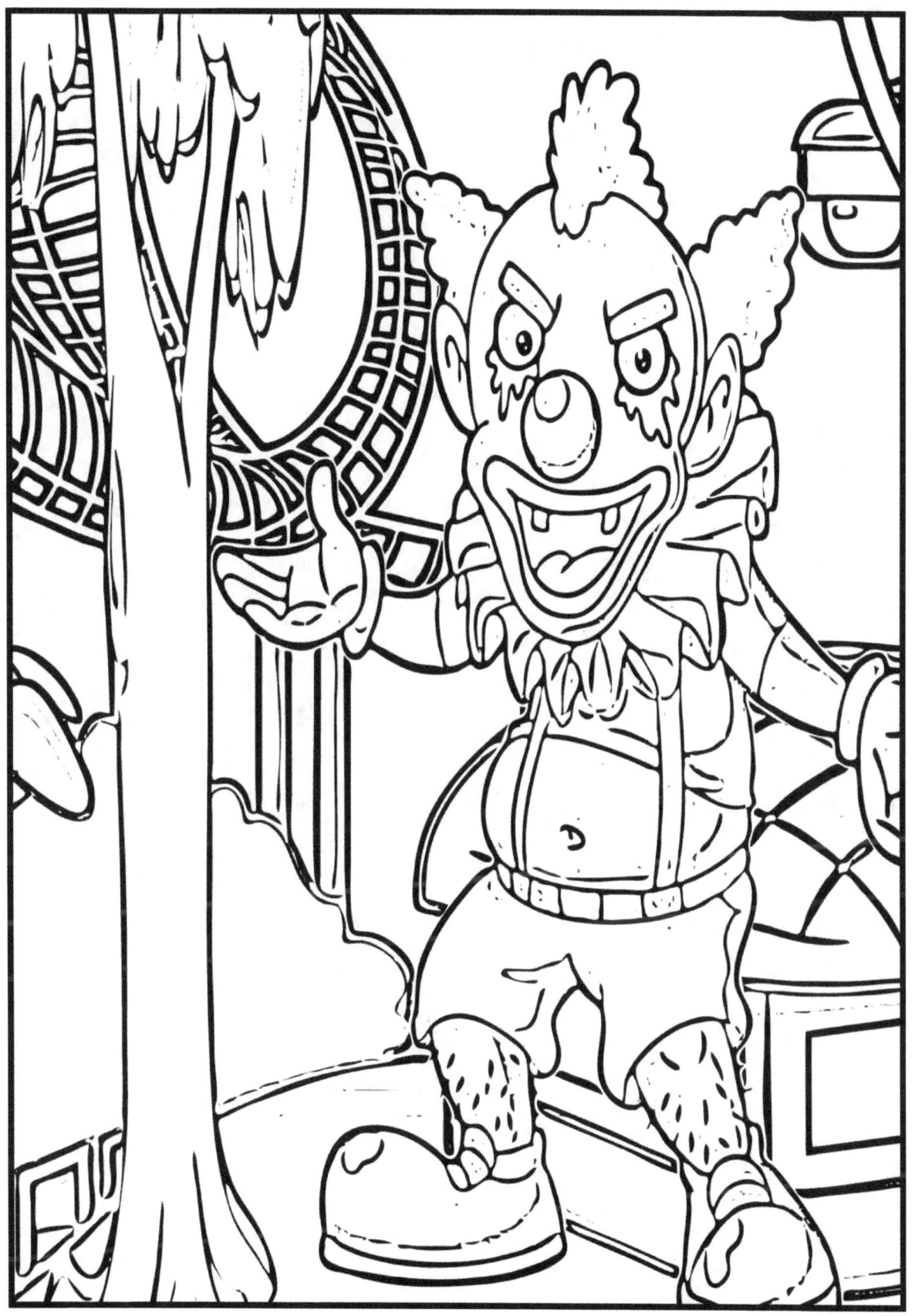

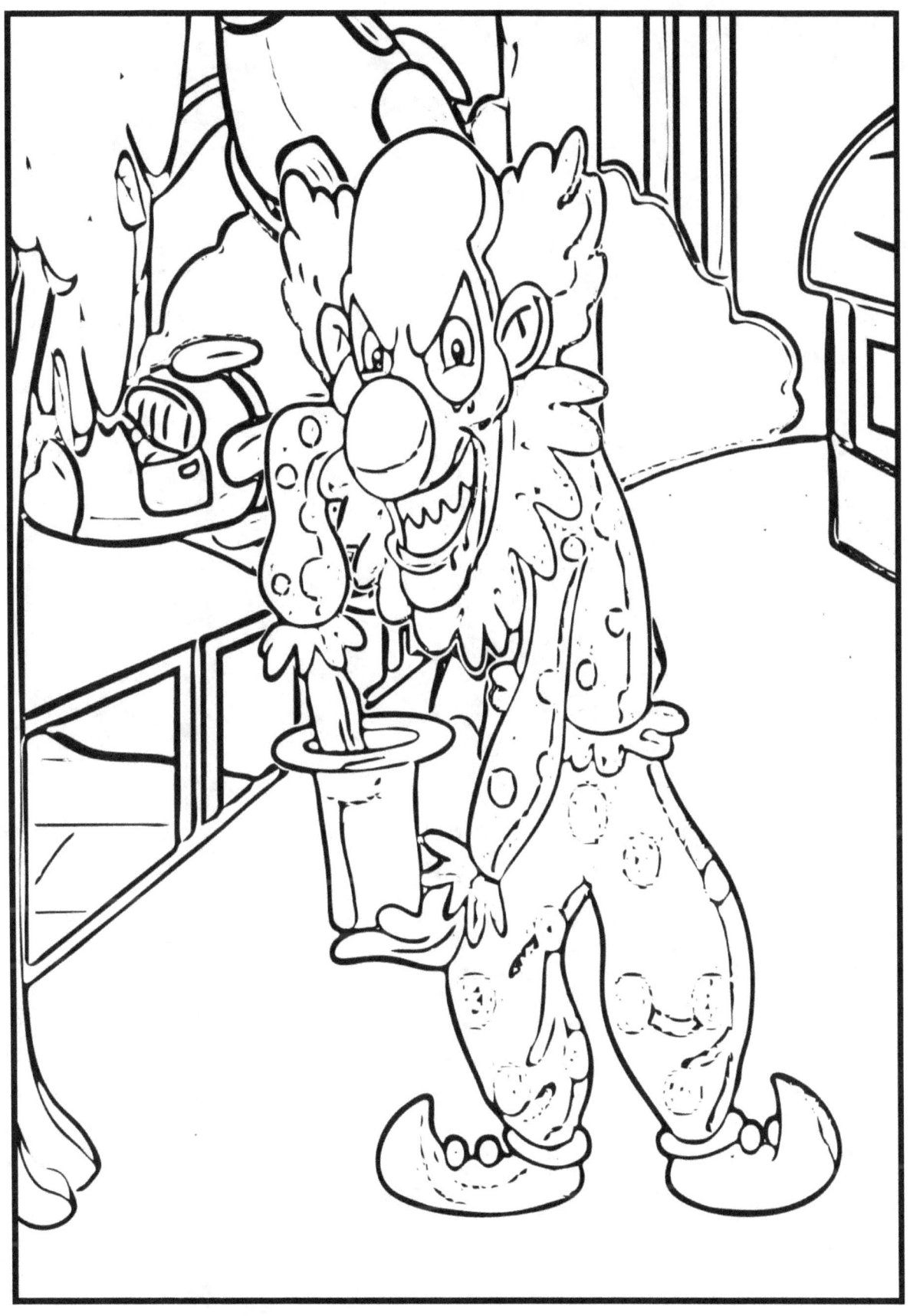

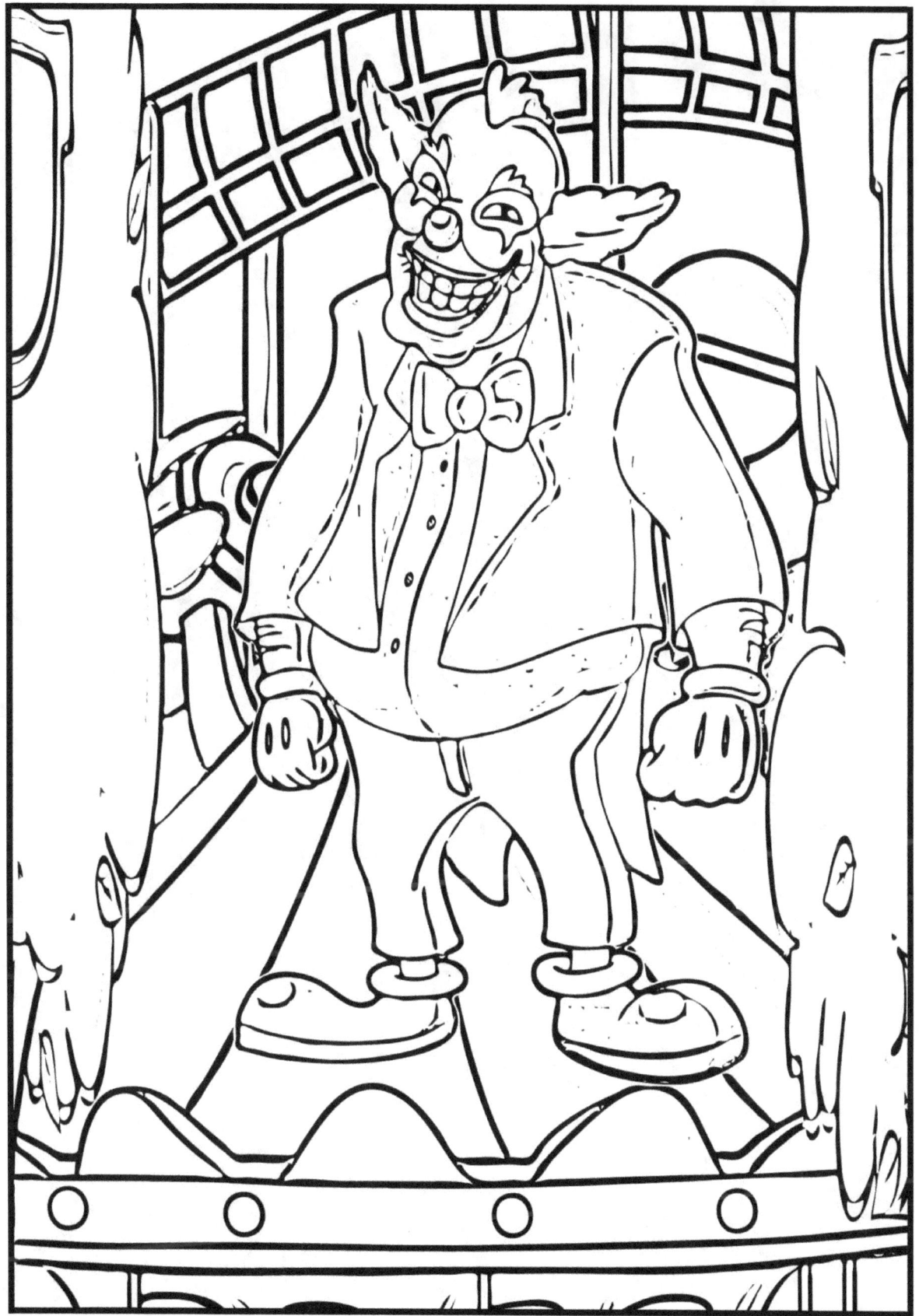

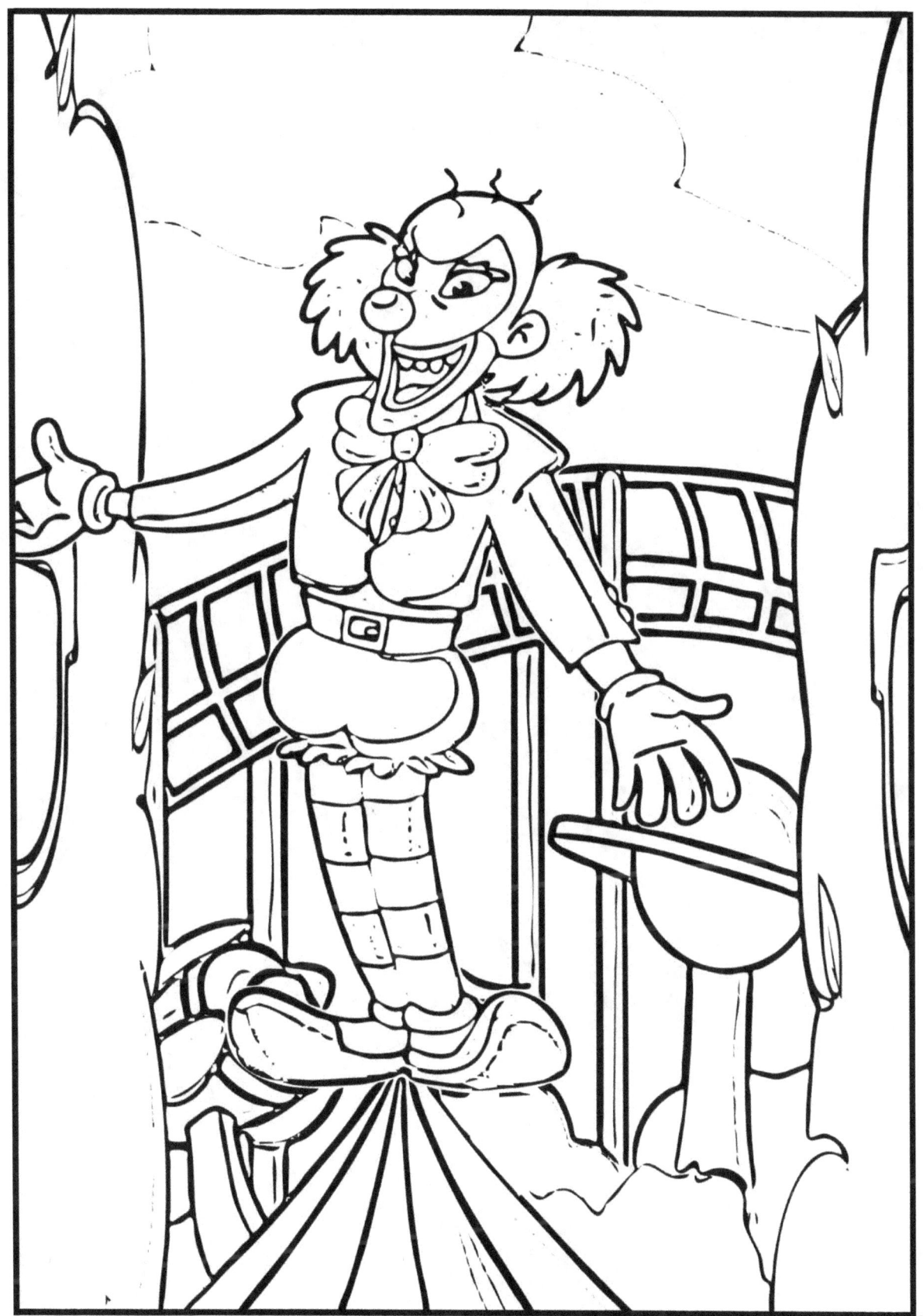

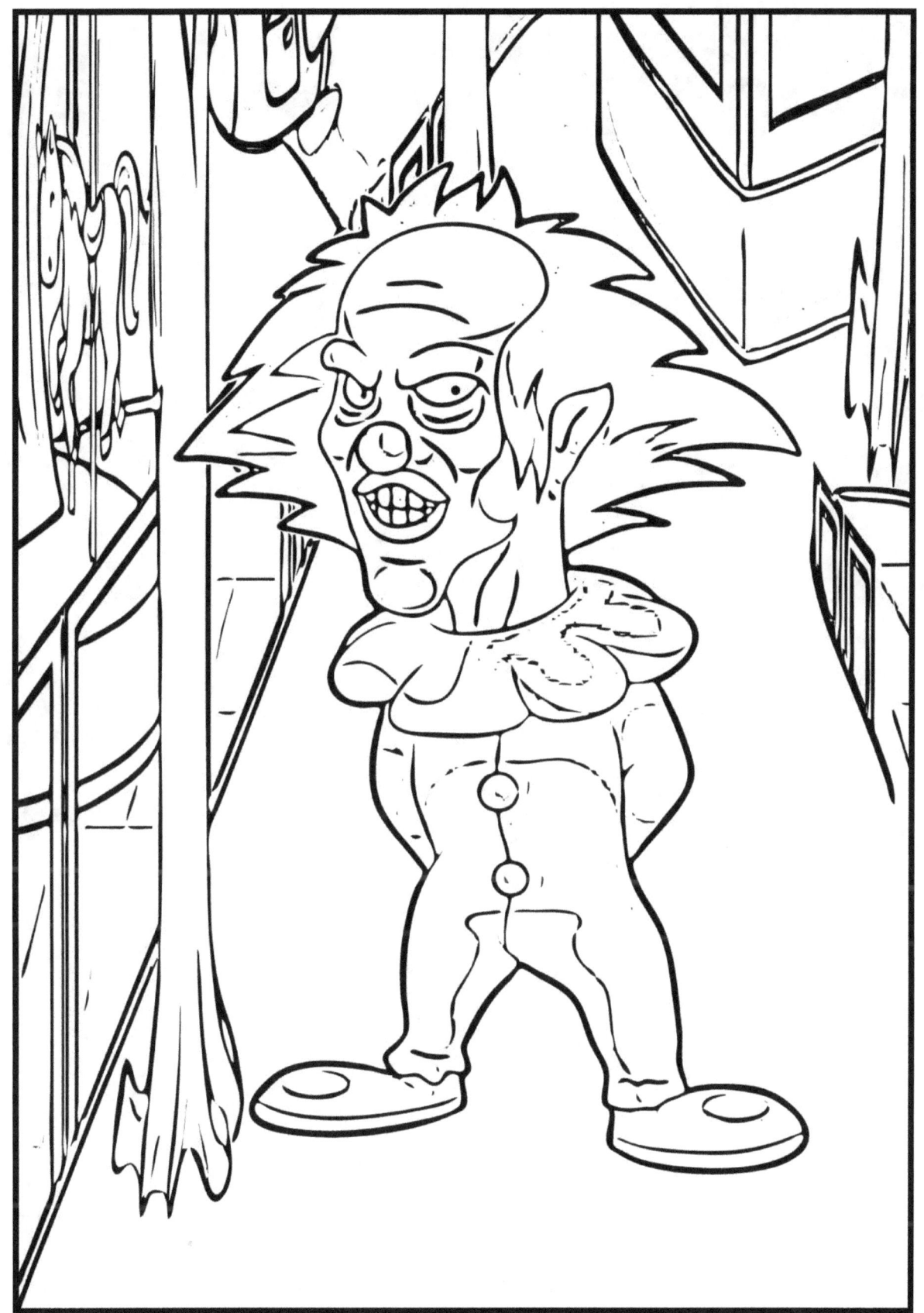

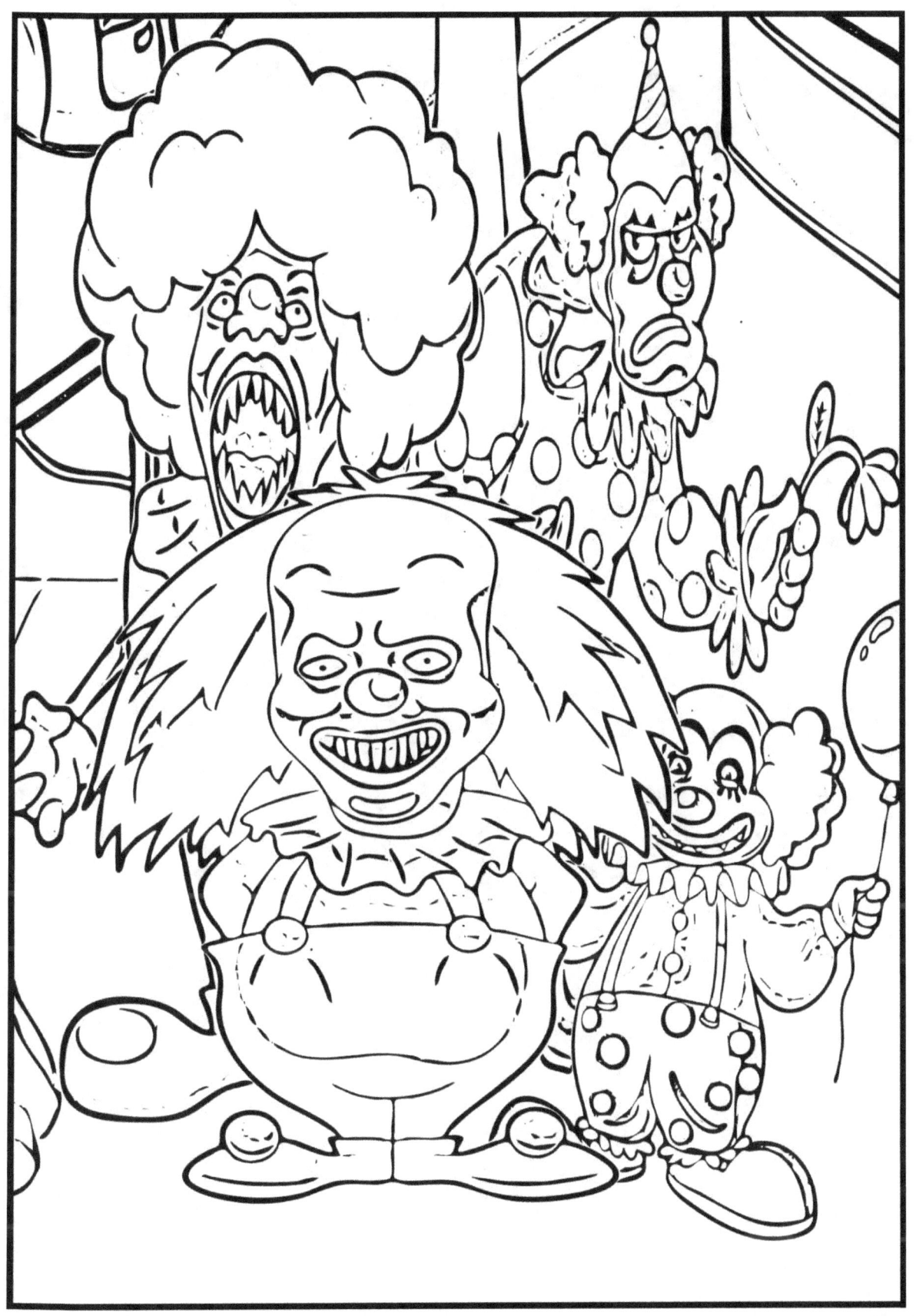

www.ingramcontent.com/pod-product-compliance
Lightning Source LLC
Chambersburg PA
CBHW081556170526
45166CB00009B/2715